Everyday Traditions

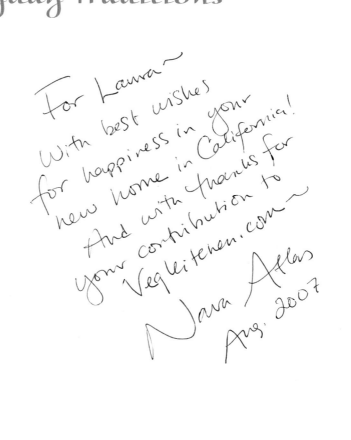

For Laura~
With best wishes
for happiness in your
new home in California!
And with thanks for
your contribution to
VegKitchen.com~

Nava Atlas
Aug. 2007

Selected books by Nava Atlas

The Vegetarian Family Cookbook
The Vegetarian 5-Ingredient Gourmet
Vegetarian Soups for All Seasons
Vegetarian Celebrations
Vegetarian Express
Vegetariana
Expect the Unexpected When You're Expecting!
(A Parody)

Everyday Traditions

Simple Family Rituals for Connection and Comfort

Written and illustrated by

Nava Atlas

Amberwood Press

Poughkeepsie, NY

Printed in China

Visit our web site at www.everydaytraditions.com

Book design and illustrations by Nava Atlas

ISBN 0-9630243-7-X

10 9 8 7 6 5 4 3 2 1

First edition

Contents

Introduction: Everyday traditions and simple rituals for a fast-paced world

In these fast-paced times, many of us hunger for simple, meaningful traditions we can pass on to our children, as well as share with family and friends. These don't have to be religious or cultural rites, or even things we recall from our own childhoods, but rather, little ways to embellish daily routines, create unique celebrations, and encourage fun activities that reflect our values and passions. Every parent I know wants to show love and affection to their children with actions as well as words. Your personal family rituals are the perfect way to do all of this and more. Beloved habits become rituals; rituals, repeated and enhanced over time, become traditions.

Ritual is a concept that can be defined in a number of ways. To some, it implies the formal observance of religious rites. To others, it suggests certain New Age practices—burning incense, drumming in a circle, chanting affirmations. In our culture and others, among the most widely observed rituals relate to life cycle passages—births, birthdays, weddings, and the like. These and familiar holiday rites may be the only rituals many of us acknowledge. One of the simplest definitions of ritual, though, is right in the dictionary: Any customarily repeated act or series of acts. To this I would add: Done with intention and attention. It's this kind of ordinary ritual that will be explored in this book—small, everyday ceremonies and personal traditions that can smooth life's rough edges, and add order and texture to the complex, busy lives of women and their families.

The repetitive, cyclical, and predictable nature of rituals is what makes them comforting and reassuring. For families, establishing daily, monthly, and annual rituals creates lasting memories and powerful bonds. Everyday rituals need not be elaborate to be meaningful. On the contrary, the simpler, the better—aren't our lives complicated enough? Personal rituals can be an antidote to the relentless busy-ness and complexity of life. By committing, for instance, to an unwavering time each night to cuddle up and read aloud to a child, you create an unspoken promise, which kept regularly, conveys to your child that he or she comes first, and that this time shared over books is important. Adding sensual elements—a cozy comforter, a warm beverage to sip, a soft light—heightens the sensory experience. This is how a familiar ritual can produce a slowed-down, in-the-moment experience that becomes extraordinary in a quiet way.

Everyday rituals that were givens not long ago are now charming anachronisms. The family dinner, one of the most basic and nourishing of daily routines, has given way to after-school sports, lessons, late meetings, long commutes, and conflicting schedules. Instead of making life simpler, technological devices and a glut of media have made it seem fragmented. Writing letters has been overtaken by e-mail and instant messaging. Pop culture has supplanted more enriching forms of entertainment. Merely making time for reading a great book or getting together regularly with friends can seem like impossible dreams for busy women.

Creating rituals around activities that give pleasure, but which we often find little time for, helps ensure that they will be part of our lives—whether interacting with good friends, enjoying meaningful family time, observing seasonal changes, reading, reflecting, or eating well. For example, we all need to eat every day. But too often, at the end of a tiring day, it's all too easy to rush highly processed or take-out meals to the table or rely on take-out. Within these pages you'll find plentiful inspiration for restoring the kitchen to its rightful place at the heart of the home, and learn how to create rituals for the daily dinner and special meals.

Many of the women who contributed stories and ideas for this book are busy mothers who were at first perplexed about the difference between routine and ritual. As Meg Cox, author of *The Heart of a Family,* so aptly puts it, "ritual is routine with sprinkles and hot sauce." A routine is something you do regularly because you need to, rather than because you choose to: You see your friends only when your frantic schedule allows; you nag your kids to get into bed; you rush up and down the aisles of the supermarket; you pile the kids into the car on Wednesdays to go to soccer practice. Here are their ritual counterparts: You participate in a monthly knitting or book group to connect with friends; you tell a story and sing two songs to your kids at bedtime; you stop at a produce market and an Italian grocery each Friday afternoon to get ingredients for an easy, festive end-of-the-week meal; you pile the kids into the car one Sunday each month for a special nature outing. The difference is that the latter group of actions are deliberate, and can be infused with personal touches that inspire anticipation.

In this book you will be invited both to rediscover the role ritual can play in daily family life, and how personal traditions can bring order to lives that can sometimes feel chaotic. In this sometimes uncomfortable era, it should come as little surprise that quite a few women find comfort in rituals that recall simpler times, such as picking produce to bake into pies, canning jam and tomatoes, or participating in knitting circles. On the other hand, we may not be able to gather for the Norman Rockwell-style Sunday supper at Grandma's, if Grandma lives three thousand miles away or prefers skiing in the Rockies to spending all day over a hot stove. But if we long for a sense of connection over food, we can participate in a regular Sunday potluck with local family members, or a monthly dinner club with friends.

Likewise, even if yesterday's coffee-klatches and mah-jongg groups have little appeal to contemporary women, "girlfriend gatherings" are as appealing as ever to busy women. With little time to just hang out, we want time shared with friends to be purposeful—discussing books, sharing cultural activities, or connecting over badly needed exercise.

Though I welcome male readers to these pages, you'll note that it is written from the female perspective; all the stories and most of the quotes are from female voices. This is by no means meant to be exclusionary; though men certainly enjoy participating in rituals, I simply found that women are far more often the ones who initiate and maintain rituals in family life and among their friends. You'll find many delightful stories of how women have tailored rituals to suit the needs of contemporary family life. Use these and the many simple ideas in these pages as a springboard to developing rituals and traditions suited to your family's needs.

It's worth taking the time to think about what everyday traditions you might have cherished as a child, and how you can pass these along to your own children. Apart from the big holiday traditions that may immediately leap to mind, recall those activities that gave you a sense of continuity and security when you were younger—the annual road trip, barbecues on the beach, weekly dinner with the grandparents, moonlit walks with your dad. Granted, for those of us who had less-than-idyllic childhoods, what's past may be best left there. If that's the case for you, give yourself the gift of an expansive blank canvas on which to create new traditions and rituals from scratch for your family and friends.

In these rapidly changing, increasingly impersonal times, everyday traditions and simple rituals can help shape and order our experiences as individuals and as a family unit. They allow us to relish and appreciate the present, rather than rushing toward whatever we think we need to do next. Incorporating rituals into daily life requires a shift in attitude and tiny sparks of inspiration rather than sizeable chunks of time. By transforming our already existing patterns and fundamental pleasures into satisfying rituals and simple ceremonies, we can cement and expand the blessings already present in our lives and more readily enhance the lives of those to whom we're connected.

Rituals and traditions—why they're great for families

Like many busy parents, I'm guilty of having given little thought to my family's traditions and rituals when my sons were small. My husband and I weren't youngsters when we plunged into parenthood. We began this journey with little role modeling, having grown up, like many of our generation, in families whose ideas about parenting were fundamentally different from ours. Who had time to think about rituals? The notion never even occurred to me, though now, of course, I wish it had.

A few winters ago, we unexpectedly found ourselves rather underscheduled. Soccer season was over, an interest in piano lessons had waned, and a long winter break loomed with no vacation plans. Once conscious of this, the four of us (my husband and I and our two sons, then in the later elementary school years) mutually agreed to make the experience more deliberate. Extracurricular activities and sports were put on hold; we ate out and went to the movies only occasionally. We did continue to see extended family and friends, though bowing to winter hibernation, not as frequently as during other times of the year.

I began to explore how I could incorporate simpler activities and pleasures into our family life. The results were more gratifying than I ever could have anticipated, and from this brief interlude, several cherished rituals emerged. Reading aloud to my sons was already a beloved family ritual, but with more time on our hands, it became a passion. For a brief but intensive time, we delved into classic fairy tales and ethnic folktales. From there, we immersed ourselves in the giddily bizarre world of Roald Dahl. Then, our read-aloud ritual continued with a focus on children's classics, including *Peter Pan, Alice in Wonderland and Through the Looking Glass,* and *Tom Sawyer*.

A longtime winter-hater, I grew fonder of the season, thanks to all the comforts we established or cemented that year. We put out a backyard bird feeder for wintering birds, and were amazed at the variety that came along. A bird book provided a fun way to identify our feathered visitors, and the boys videotaped each variety. Getting snowshoes provided an incentive for walking in the snow (I was actually disappointed that we had so little snow the winter following). Of course, coming in and sitting by the fire with tea or cocoa afterwards is what makes snowshoeing more of a winter ritual than a sport. We also initiated a tradition of buying a large jigsaw puzzle at the beginning of each winter to work on slowly throughout the season, especially during snow days.

An interest in baking homemade quick breads, cookies, and muffins flourished that year. My younger son was nearly always in the kitchen with me, and together, we developed a repertoire of delicious and healthy baked goods. Baking with my younger son became a favorite ritual for stormy days. By the age of eleven, he became an accomplished baker in his own right. Though we have never since been as underscheduled as we were that one wonderful winter, many of the traditions we established then have carried forward into each successive winter.

I still dread some aspects of winter, but having some cozy rituals to look forward to makes the season more fun and less daunting. We were also inspired to designate traditions for each of our distinct seasons here in the northeastern United States, though oddly, none as cherished as those we enjoy during our least favorite season.

Rituals are repeated patterns of meaningful acts. If you are mindful of your actions, you will see the ritual patterns. If you see the patterns, you may understand them. If you understand them, you may enrich them. In this way, the habits of a lifetime become sacred.

—Robert Fulghum,
From Beginning to End

Discovering the joys of ritual and tradition when we had a bit more free and open time did not make me feel like any sort of expert. On the contrary, it made me feel sad that this discovery didn't happen until my sons were well out of early childhood. That said, it's never too late to initiate rituals. Even teens can benefit greatly from family traditions, and given the right cues, can be of great help in initiating and maintaining them. My curiosity led me to explore the subject further, talking to friends about their own rituals and traditions.

As the author of several books on vegetarian cooking, I hope you won't mind a partiality to food rituals in these pages; after all, everyone likes to eat, and food always has played a starring role in many traditions, large and small. Perhaps if I were more athletic, I would have included more traditions revolving around sports, but as things stand, we spend more time around the kitchen table than at the baseball field, and you'll notice that emphasis in the pages of this book.

William J. Doherty, Ph.D., points out in *The Intentional Family* that rituals enhance many of those activities that you already engage in: "You have to feed your children, so start with improving the quality of those feeding rituals, without lengthening the time. You have to put your kids to bed; work on making it more pleasurable. You probably have birthday parties, holiday celebrations, and countless family activities." Exploring the possibilities for enhancing these ordinary activities makes a world of difference when we distinguish routine from ritual.

✧ Rituals help give order and rhythm to a child's day. Parenting experts agree that the predictability and repetition of daily rituals makes for more secure children. Family dinner, the walk to school, a young child's bath, bedtime stories—these common rituals, if not particularly original or exciting, convey to a child that even the simplest of daily activities can be times for comfort and connection.

✧ Rituals help ease daily transitions. The transition from wakefulness to sleep, for example, is especially challenging for young children and their exhausted parents; special rituals make going to bed fun, rather than stressful (see Sweet Dreams, page 36). The daily transition of parting can be made less daunting with a group hug, special handshakes, or secret signals.

✧ Rituals give families various ways to express love. These can include how you greet one another in the morning, or how you say good night; how you care for one another when someone is sick or has had a difficult day; the unique ways you show appreciation for each member of the family; or simply the ways and frequency with which you verbalize "I love you." Though many of us practice daily rituals without being conscious of them, they are more delightful when deliberate.

✧ Rituals reinforce tradition. Whether part of a larger framework (such as faith or community) or personal to the individual family, traditions—as long as they remain meaningful and pleasurable and not rote or obligatory—are the footprint of each family's history. They gently recall the past while rooting us in the present.

✧ Traditions link generations. Carrying traditions forward helps children feel more connected to their extended family. Maybe you bake the same cookies that your mother and grandmother did; or you celebrate a grandparent's birthday by gathering and telling well-worn but beloved family stories each year. Perhaps you pull out an old family photo album on a particular anniversary or birthday. Any such simple rituals can be an enchanting link to the past.

✧ Everyday rituals express family values without judgment or preaching. A family that loves the arts can set up monthly outings to art museums, and decide in advance on interesting activities to do while there. Parents who cherish nature can introduce their children to special places to explore and revisit each season. Families who wish to teach the value of giving can create rituals around volunteering and donating.

It's best to remain flexible where family rituals are concerned. As your children grow, they may no longer need a bedtime story, but might still appreciate having you sit with them for a quiet chat or a back rub at bedtime. Some rituals dwindle naturally, while others evolve into something new. Others remain firmly rooted as kids grow older. If a ritual begins meeting with resistance, it's time to let go; once it feels forced, it's no more fun than any other obligation.

My own discovery of everyday traditions and ordinary rituals grew from the unexpected gift of more open time. But I believe that awareness is more crucial than great swathes of time for recognizing and finding regular time for them in the course of any busy life. They don't add to your "to-do" list, but rather, give you a sense that more time is being created in the midst of your busy life. By deciding what's important, creating little pockets of time becomes surprisingly easy.

It's stating the obvious that many kids today are overscheduled, rushed, and sometimes stressed by too much activity. Rituals create islands of calm and predictability, perfect antidotes to overstuffed schedules. We don't need more "downtime" in order to create rituals; rather, rituals actually become the downtime we all crave, whether it's sharing stories each night, having a pizza-and-movie night once a week, hiking alongside a waterfall each spring, or enjoying a memorable birthday celebration every year. Family rituals and traditions are the simplest yet strongest forms of connection and comfort for all involved, and can undoubtedly be the basis of our children's fondest memories.

Everyday Traditions

Part one

In the kitchen and at the table

*One of the primary ways we connect with each other is by eating together. . . .
Much of our fundamental well-being comes from the basic reassurance that there
is a place for us at the table. We belong here. Here we are served and we serve
others. Here we give and receive sustenance. No small matter.*

—Edward Espe Brown, *Tomato Blessings and Radish Teachings*

family dinner at the table: Reconsidering an endangered ritual

Cooking and eating offer abundant opportunities to bring rituals of comfort and pleasure into daily life, simply because we all need to eat every day. Yet, often, they're missed opportunities, as frozen entrées, makeshift meals, and take-out menus call to our craving for convenience. No wonder so many Western cultures have become overfed and undernourished. Serving fresh food that's been prepared with love (or at least a good attitude) and seasoned with camaraderie is a simple formula for nourishing both body and spirit on a daily basis.

Some ingredients for daily dinner at the table

According to a number of studies, about 30 percent fewer American families eat dinner together today than they did twenty years ago. Still, other polls paint a less dire picture: A Roper poll done in the nineties indicated that slightly more than half of American families eat together five or more times per week; other polls paint a somewhat less optimistic picture, showing that only about a third eat together regularly. Contrast this with a report sent to the *International Herald-Tribune* in early 2004, asserting that in France, 75 percent of families currently eat dinner together. I suspect that this number is similar in other European and Asian cultures that value the tradition of sharing meals. Let's take a page from the global community and rediscover a sustaining tradition.

With work schedules, lessons, and sports practices pulling family members in all directions just as the day should be winding down, it's no wonder fewer families are finding the time to eat together. Yet, at the same time, it's encouraging to know that many others are making a great effort to keep this ritual alive.

Studies have been done comparing children and teens who have regular family dinners at home with those who don't. The results are consistent, and striking. Teens from families who eat dinner together are less likely to use illegal drugs, alcohol, and cigarettes than teenagers who rarely eat dinner with their parents. Another practical (if predictable) perk is that children who have regular, at-home dinners eat meals that are healthier and include more vegetables. In addition, children who have regular family dinners are believed to fare better in school. Few daily rituals offer better opportunity to connect, converse, share, and feel nourished.

What's on the table and how it's presented speaks volumes about our willingness to give mealtime rituals the place they so richly deserve in daily life. Don't buy into the myth that it's too time consuming to put a decent dinner on the table regularly. Still, meals aren't only about the food on the table. The setting, atmosphere, stories, and conversations that accompany the food all contribute to making even the most ordinary meal memorable. Consider:

✧ Is your kitchen the heart of the home, or the center of the cyclone? Because of its central location in most homes and apartments, kitchens often become repositories for mail, bills, school notices, homework, recent purchases, newspapers, unfinished projects, toys, and more. Make sure your kitchen suggests food and comfort, not clutter and chaos. Some suggest that it is more the attitude one brings to the kitchen than its decor that matters; it can become, to some degree, a sacred space. "Thinking of your kitchen as a temple may be just what you need to bring more harmony into your life," suggest Robin Robertson and Jon Robertson, authors of *The Sacred Kitchen*. The kitchen should be comfortable, functional, and as clutter free as possible. Give it some sensuous elements, plus some hint of the season.

✧ Do your shopping habits contribute positively or negatively to your attitude toward meal preparation? Do you plan your meals and pantry needs so that shopping can be at least a pleasant, if not downright enjoyable routine, and not on a par with going to the dentist? Does your food shopping include planned stops at farm stands and organic produce markets, quality bakeries, and ethnic food shops? If you find yourself frantically prowling the aisles of crowded supermarkets without a list in hand, or if you wait until there is literally nothing in the house with which to make a simple meal, then you need to rethink your shopping habits. For more ideas, see Seasonal food pleasures, page 102.

✧ If your meals are primarily shared with a partner, how do the two of you make them significant? Are you using them as a time to connect after a busy day and catch up with one another, or do you chow down over the mail or evening news? Couples who spend long days apart might consider how they can create regular mealtimes that aren't merely a time to eat, but a way to reconnect. See how one couple turned the daily dilemma of "whose turn is it to cook?" into a relaxing shared ritual on page 15.

✧ Do you bond over food regularly with extended family and/or friends? Plenty of families still hold to the tradition of a weekly Sabbath meal (the Friday night Shabbat dinner of the Jewish faith, the

after-church Sunday dinner practiced by many Christians).
Yet others enjoy regular extended family meals as a matter
of course, without the structure of faith. Casting a wide net
of family connection with food as the common denomina-
tor is one of the most time-honored ways to connect, and an
ideal way to have cousins grow up together, to see aunts and
uncles, siblings, and grandparents without having to make
separate plans.

Amy's grandparents, Italian immigrants who settled in the
New York City suburbs (with four offspring), retained certain
cultural values that kept their family together, while in other
ways assimilating. A Friday night pizza dinner (with every
part of the pizza made from scratch by Amy's grandmother)
has been, as Amy puts it, "a family institution." When Amy
was growing up, it was a way to play with cousins and visit
with aunts and uncles. As a teen, she sometimes resented having to participate, but now, as a young woman, she claims she
wouldn't miss this gathering for the world. And the homemade pizza is a must. Once, her grandmother decided to skip
the pizza and serve turkey, which sent the family into shock!
That never happened again.

✧ Finally, have you begun any food traditions for your children that will foster warm memories and a healthy relationship with food for your children as they grow up? Hopefully,
they won't leave home only with recollections of the take-out
menu drawer and cereal cabinet! Comfort food: Soothing traditions, starting on page 18, may inspire you to create great
food memories to pass along.

Doing dinner:
Confessions of a radical mother

According to a recent article in *Time* magazine, groups of harried parents across the U.S. are joining a wave of slow-living advocates by doing something really revolutionary—having one sit-down dinner at home with their kids each week. I don't know whether to applaud or cry. The idea that parents are willing to undertake the Herculean task of rearranging their schedules to fit in a single dinner at home is laudable. The fact that it requires superhuman effort is terribly sad.

People in Europe or Latin America are horrified to hear of families in the U.S. gulping down dinner in their cars on a daily basis. In cultures where families gather for meals every afternoon and again late in the evening, they view this obsession with achievement as baffling, alarming, and pitiful.

When I tell people that I have four teenage daughters (ages thirteen, fourteen, sixteen, and seventeen), they look at me with a mixture of horror and pity. Life must be tough at your house, they say. You must live in your car, they tell me. Um—no. My family eats a relaxing dinner together at home—by candle-light!—at least five nights a week. It's the best part of the day.

Don't get me wrong. Sports are great for kids. So is drama. And music. And debate. But dinner matters, too. I figure that my kids aren't going to be living with us forever, and while they're here, it's a lot more important to have dinner together than it is to have the girls sign up for every sport and activity on earth. Here's a typical scene at our house: four girls sprawled on the floor in front of the fireplace, doing homework or reading. This is after we've had an enjoyable dinner and they've cleaned up the kitchen.

It's not that my kids don't do anything. They're into all kinds of activities—drama, music, dance, volunteer work, and even jobs. Two are gearing up for lacrosse, one is in the midst of interviews for a yearlong exchange program; the oldest is in her senior year and doing college applications. It's a busy time. All of us—singles, married couples, young families and empty nesters—can benefit from the dinner ritual. By adopting and continuing the tradition of shared meals and conversation, we are emphasizing the importance of thinking and sharing ideas. If we want our culture to value thinking, we've got to start by offering a tribute to it on a daily basis.

Okay, so my kids may never get athletic scholarships. They may never meet a single university athletic director before choosing which college to attend. They won't be the next Olympic gymnast or ice-skater, and they're not likely to be conducting symphonies by the time they're twenty five. They'll have to settle for being happy, smart, kind, aware, motivated, and full of enthusiasm for the world and their place in it. Their father and I will just have to be satisfied with lasting memories of slow life with our cherished children, and our daughters will strive only to duplicate this same lifestyle for their own families someday.

Radical, isn't it?

—Maya Talisman Frost

Of all the rooms in our lives, the kitchen can feed the soul and become a comforting place to be at any time of day. I think of the kitchen as a gathering place, a place for shared comforts, for mutual efforts at preparing good meals with loving care.

—Alexandra Stoddard, *Living a Beautiful Life*

Making the table a welcoming place

Set the table, set the tone: It takes little effort to make the table look welcoming with dishes and utensils that you and your family enjoy using. This may not seem like a major point, but like the three bowls used at Buddhist monasteries, they are an intrinsic part of the experience. The tableware you use should be both functional and interesting: ceramic dishes that lend an earthy flair to the table, jazzy colorful plates, or vintage dishes that belonged to your grandmother. Maybe your little ones can have their own special plates—small, colorful dishware might help them enjoy the dinner ritual that much more. Some families use certain dishes or a special candlestick only when all are able to be present at the table. Fresh flowers, a seasonal centerpiece, colorful napkins—all these little touches help bring attention to what is before us. From a young age, children can set the dinner table. Allow them some creative freedom, within reason, and encourage them to include personal and seasonal touches. A little whimsy adds to the spirit of a shared meal.

Have a beginning and ending: A signal that the meal is about to begin, such as lighting candles or reciting a blessing, helps create a framework for the experience. Teach your kids to respect the cook by waiting to take the first bite until he or she is seated. As soon as it's realistic to do so, get children into the habit of sitting through the meal until everyone is done, but be flexible. Better to let your little ones go off and play rather than get restless at the table; likewise, if your adolescents are inundated with schoolwork, don't require them to sit for undue time at the table. The end of the meal can be signaled by thanking the cook and cleaning up together. Make sure that everyone participates in cleanup; even those who left the table earlier should come back and pitch in.

Engage the senses: Rounding up the family and putting a nourishing meal on the table daily is challenging enough, to be sure. But once you establish a comfortable routine, you can begin to transform dinner from routine to ritual. By engaging the senses, even ordinary meals can be memorable. The beauty of candles or flowers at the table, the snap and crunch of a raw vegetable platter, the surprising lilt of a fruit salsa or chutney on the plate, the scent of fresh bread, the touch of hands joined around the table for a moment of gratitude—these are but a few ways to add to the pleasure of eating with a few easy nods to the senses.

Sit and chat: Ideally, of course, the dinner table should be a place for conversation and connection. The reality is that by the time we sit down to the evening meal, many of us (especially if younger children are involved) feel too weary for sparkling repartee. It helps to provide a common thread from day to day, such as going around the table and having everyone talk about the highlight of their day. Dinnertime is for checking in, exchanging news, and enjoying good food and one another's company.

Having a set of prompts in mind works well to spark conversation. Discuss an interesting news story or community event, or have everyone talk about the high point of their day. My older son recently suggested that we occasionally celebrate

As long as we have to make dinner anyway, let it be a celebration of life, a haven of quality time, and a sacred act that celebrates the connection between cooking and our spiritual health.

—Robin Robertson
and Jon Robertson,
The Sacred Kitchen

or commemorate something that happened on that date—a significant historic event, or the birthday of a person we admire. Many web sites—for example, www.infoplease.com —have such listings.

If you want to keep conversation light, try "conversation-in-a-jar," suggested by Meg Cox in *The Book of New Family Traditions*. Prepare a container to be set on the table, containing strips of paper marked with open-ended statements such as "The strangest thing that happened to me today was . . ." or "The best book I've read recently is. . . ."

Explore blessings: Many families enjoy starting the meal with some sort of blessing; others find this feels rather awkward. Some report that saying a blessing can at first feel forced, but after a while, it becomes a calming way to begin a meal. If you'd like to explore this idea in a less conventional way, consider going outside your personal tradition with blessings from other cultures. Chinese, Indian, Native American, Tibetan, Irish, and others have lovely blessings that can be adopted—or adapted! A few lines from a favorite poem can also be an offbeat way to open your meal. *Saying Grace: Blessings for the Family Table* (edited by Sarah McElwain) is a little book filled with ideas from world religious traditions, great poets, Aesop, and even cowboys.

Be flexible and realistic: If your family's schedule simply won't allow for dinner at the table every night, try to carve out the time for at least some meals together. If it's only twice a week, so be it; make the most of those meals together. And in truth, it's unrealistic to expect relaxing family meals with

We eat dinner together each day and always give thanks for our food, saying the same prayer each time, with each person saying their little bit. Then we go around again, and each adds a personal entry, giving thanks for something positive that affected us during the day—anything from seeing the sun or having a friend over, to getting some work done, or having a good day at school.

—Carlie Graves

On the first night of a new month at dinner, we read that month's page from a book called *Be Blest,* by Mary Beth Owens, which has a prayer for each month. It's a way of trying to be mindful of the changing seasons and the special things about every month.

—Reed Mangels

toddlers, babies, and tired young children. When my sons were toddlers and preschoolers, I often fed them dinner early so that my husband and I could enjoy a quiet meal. We kept revisiting the concept of eating as a family at regular intervals as they grew up. Gradually, a full-fledged family dinner evolved. Generally, kids are ready for the dinner ritual once they are school age. Remember, rigid food rituals are hardly better than no rituals at all.

Candles at the table: Candles are often saved for special occasions, though their soothing glow provides an easy way to elevate the nightly meal. The simple act of lighting candles gives the meal a definite beginning; older children enjoy this task. Dinner is over when the candles are blown out—the perfect "job" for little ones.

Candles are most welcome during the dark days of the year. For casual daily meals, try short, chunky candles or colorful tapers in ceramic holders. It's also fun to set a tiny tea light at everyone's place. Send a long, safe candle around so everyone can light their individual candle. When the meal is over, everyone blows out their own candle. While hardly a revolutionary idea, candles can sharpen the focus of a family dinner, while softening the atmosphere.

Dedicating candles

We have a candle-lighting ceremony at the dinner table each night that our family loves. The oldest member (my husband, Mark), lights a candle and dedicates it to a cause or a person, or says a prayer. Each member of the family takes a turn in the following nights, one night at a time. Only one new candle is lit each night. After everyone has had a turn, the process begins again. As each new candle is lit, the old ones are lit also, and remembered. When we started this ritual, Mark dedicated the first candle to my father, for his ninety years of life. The next night, I lit a candle for two emotionally damaged kids in the class that I teach. Ian's candle was to stop hunger. Coulter's was for me, for all that I do.

After that, we began four new candles, one night at a time, and revisited our old candles. After we each had dedicated three candles, we started a new set of dedications. We recently had twelve candles lit on our table at dinner, and they were so beautiful. It gives us a chance to combine giving, loving thoughts, and an action.

We have our candle ceremony after dinner due to the practicalities of hunger and not wanting to eat cold food. The ceremony can be a little lengthy, and we are in a more mellow mood after a meal. The intent was to do the ceremony every night, but due to the kids' sports and music involvement, we are not all at home during dinner every night. So, we light candles every time that we can all come together for an evening meal.

This ceremony becomes a wonderfully potent and useful structure within which we can express feelings, thoughts, desires, and dreams that add a new level of communication and sharing. This has enriched the soul of our family. The beauty of the candles alone seems to engender beautiful and sacred thoughts and expressions, and have a positive transformational effect on any negative moods that we may have developed from the stresses of the day.

—Barbara McPhail

Cooking together

In *A Bite Off Mama's Plate: Mothers' and Daughters' Connections Through Food,* author Miriam Meyers portrays the kitchen as a feminine world of activity and communication. Whether the stories of mothers and daughters in the kitchen take place in the past or present (helping, learning, or often just talking as Mom cooked, baked, and canned), they carry an air of nostalgia. One woman describes the fun of helping with the weekly baking of pies, donuts, and breads with her mother and grandmother on Saturday mornings. I would have thought this activity some-what of a relic, had I not personally met a mother and her two twenty-something daughters who bake and cook together on Saturdays, not out of necessity, but as a pleasurable ritual.

Cooking together has gone beyond the traditional paradigm of daughters learning at their mothers' apron strings, and fortunately, is no longer limited to the females in the family. Some families have developed rituals for cooking as a team, whether for daily dinner or for fun and relaxation, often with male partners and sons as equal participants. Sometimes, the daily necessity of getting a meal on the table can feel like a lonely task when it is the domain of just one cook. When you involve your partner or children in the process of creating meals, you also create a perfect opportunity to pass down food customs and share culinary passions.

Cooking together as a couple can be an antidote to stress. When Gina and John were first married, each had a small business. In spite of their hectic schedules, they tried to avoid falling into the habit of eating out every night. They decided that

My mother made beautiful Southern biscuits regularly. I sat in the kitchen talking with her as she spooned what seemed to be a random amount of self-rising flour into a special bowl, scooped a piece of fat from a can and placed it in the center of the flour, poured in buttermilk, and worked the mass with her fingers. When the dough was "right," I watched her shape the biscuits, then place them on a greased baking sheet, blackened from many years' use. I could make those biscuits today easily, though Mama never taught me formally. Being in the presence of my mother, talking with her as she made biscuits, "taught" me.

—Miriam Meyers,
*A Bite Off
Mama's Plate*

whoever got home first would make or start dinner. As is typical of small businesses, crises arose, and the temptation to see one more client or customer was ever present, often keeping them at work longer than they would have liked. Stumbling home exhausted around 9:30 or 10:00, each arrived thinking the other had already started dinner. Finally, reality set in—what a stressful way to end stressful days! The couple decided to set a time and meet in the kitchen each evening to prepare dinner together. First, they walked their dog, using the time to vent frustrations they had met with that day. This left them more relaxed for the process of preparing dinner.

Gina and John enjoy improvising with what's in the fridge and pantry. While this might not work for busy families, for them, it's part of the fun of cooking together. With dinner made, and the stresses of the day behind them, a candlelit table awaits, allowing the pair to enjoy quiet conversation over a meal prepared together.

When little ones are in the picture, many harried parents feel that they need to somehow keep them busy and out from underfoot while they throw together a quick meal. Jennifer, however, had her kids cook with her from the time they were young. When her son was very small, she got him a play stove and allowed him to "cook" using safe utensils. After her daughter came along and the kids got older, she gave them age-appropriate tasks to help prepare the meal. Jennifer admits that having her children cook with her made the process a little messier and lengthier, but they got the message that she was completely present with them.

Even if you don't cook meals with your family every day, sharing some cooking activities helps create memorable comfort food rituals. My younger son and I figured out how to make extremely good and fairly easy filled chocolates, so we consider chocolate making our personal tradition for special occasions. We've long enjoyed baking together, too. Baking is a perfect kitchen activity to share with kids, since the steps are relatively easy, and the results are delectable. This skill can be passed along to your children from a very early age and developed into a shared pastime. For Peggy, baking with her daughters, Katherine and Annie, has long been a shared passion that continues as the girls have become young women. At twenty, Katherine, her younger daughter, can hardly remember a time when she didn't bake with her mother and older sister. All of seven years old when she attempted her first solo baking venture, the jelly roll cake she made for family breakfast was a complete success.

After Annie left for college, school breaks meant coming home and spending time in the kitchen with her mother and sister, especially for holiday and special occasion meals. Now, post-college and living on her own, many Saturdays still find Annie visiting home, continuing the tradition of baking and cooking as a trio. Mornings are for baking something sweet yet healthful together, like banana-nut bread or carrot cake. After the baking is done, the three decide what they want to make for dinner. Sometimes they pore over cookbooks, make lists, and shop for ingredients; other times, they shop first and improvise later. Either way, the entire process is pleasurable and relaxing.

To hear Katherine tell it, the common bond of cooking something delicious and innovative that is suitable for their meatless diet is surpassed only by how happy they are to be in the kitchen together. Their delectable dishes are shared with their father and their teenage brother, who, though not completely in tune with the healthy food philosophy of the women in the family, are beginning to come around. Whether making meals together, or cooking recreationally, lessons learned around the kitchen counter last a lifetime.

Resources

Cooking Time Is Family Time: Cooking Together, Eating Together, and Spending Time Together by Lynn Fredericks (HarperCollins, 1999) is all about the art of cooking and eating together as a family.

Honest Pretzels: And 64 Other Amazing Recipes for Kids Ages 8 and Up by Mollie Katzen (Tricycle Press, 1999). Here's one of the best books around for budding chefs who want to cook independently for their families.

A long time ago it occurred to me that when people are tired and hungry, which in adult life is much of the time, they do not want to be confronted by an intellectually challenging meal: they want to be consoled.

When life is hard and the day has been long, the ideal dinner is not four perfect courses . . . but rather something comforting and savory, easy on the digestion—something that makes one feel, if even for only a minute, that one is safe.

—Laurie Colwin,
Home Cooking

Comfort foods: Soothing traditions

From an infant's first sip of milk, the connection between sustenance and security is forged. Comfort food is the edible equivalent of a security blanket—soothing and delightfully childish. Often bland, soft, creamy, warm, meltingly sweet, or even mushy, comfort food can calm and console before taking a single bite.

If you're a bit blue or under the weather, complex flavors that ordinarily delight may not be just what you need. A dollop of mashed potatoes or a bowl of noodle soup might do your spirit more good than any spicy delicacy seasoned with cilantro, garlic, or jalapeño peppers. And let's be perfectly clear—food as a comfort is not the same as food as a fix. Downing an entire bag of oily, salty chips or box of cookies doesn't equal the conscious savoring of "nursery foods" that trigger nostalgic connections to special people and simpler times. Comfort food is a respite, not a compulsion.

While the all-American definition of comfort food is fairly universal (macaroni and cheese; rice pudding; soups and stews; cookies, brownies, and pies; fresh muffins and biscuits; mashed potatoes, pot pie, stuffing, and other "grandma" food), in reality it's quirkier, more personal, and reflects one's ethnic roots. No one, regardless of current food preferences, waxes nostalgic about big bowls of steamed broccoli or crisp salads.

And for every woman who regaled me with a great comfort food memory, another drew a blank, myself included. Having rebelled against my childhood foods, my notions seem to have been drawn from memories of perfect 1950s TV moms—June

Cleaver serving freshly baked cookies to "The Beaver" after school, Donna Reed swirling gracefully into the dining room with fluffy mashed potatoes. But having no such traditions from my past has inspired me to create new ones for my children. You might consider doing so, too.

Creamy or noodle-filled soups, homemade macaroni and cheese, and our beloved repertoire of wholesome baked goods are among the comforts I'm convinced will follow my sons into adulthood. I hope they'll also remember sitting on high stools in the kitchen helping to stir batters, the scent of chocolate coming from the oven, and having me read *Calvin and Hobbes* aloud as they enjoyed freshly baked brownies.

The stories gathered here demonstrate how memory and senses become entwined, conjuring up the comfort foods that become part of our family history. The cozy food memories are most always connected with a special person (usually a parent or grandmother), and often, a ritual connected with the making or eating of the food.

✧ While growing up, Geetha's parents regularly made *idli* (steamed rice cakes, eaten plain or with butter and sugar) for her. A traditional Indian comfort food served for soothing major ailments and minor maladies, *idli* are also a cherished Sunday breakfast treat, much as pancakes are in Western kitchens. Geetha now makes

It seems to me that our three basic needs, for food and security and love, are so entwined that we cannot think of one without the other.

—M.F.K. Fisher

idli for her young daughter, Indira, who enthusiastically eats them out of hand. Making them is no small project; they even require special cooking equipment. But, Geetha says, *idli* evoke such comforting memories that making them for her daughter "is just one of those things that, busy as I am, I've chosen to do anyway."

✧ Proving that personal notions of comfort food are unique, two sisters, Robin and Leah, grew up in the same house and ate the same bland Eastern European Jewish food. Robin never liked it, and today, as a raw food enthusiast, politely rebuffs her mother's cajoling. For Leah, on the other hand, returning home to matzo ball soup, sweet potato *tzimmes,* and noodle pudding (which she does about once a month) makes her feel as well cared for as when she was young and her biggest worry was which jumper to wear to school. "I never cook this way at home," says Robin, who favors salads and rice dishes, "but it's not just the food. It's about how in Mom's world, so little has changed—the rosebud wallpaper in the dining room, the doilies on the end tables, the aromas, and the friendly nagging to eat a just a little more when I'm ready to burst. It's a welcome relief from my stressful job."

✧ Karen loved visiting her Norwegian grandparents for Christmas in the Midwest as a child. Her grandmother always baked *kringlas*—a traditional pastry formed into a sort of figure eight, which Karen would wash down with cinnamon-scented hot cocoa. These were served with a special plate and cup set that were just for Karen's use when she came to visit. "They had bunnies around the rim—or were they kitties?" she mused. Though the recollection has grown fuzzy, she acknowledges that the plate and cup were crucial to the ritual. For fifteen years now, Karen has baked several batches of *kringlas* during the holiday season to give as hostess gifts and to serve to guests. No bunny or kitty dishes are involved, but she does use her grandmother's original recipe.

✧ Olive learned to cook the old-fashioned way—at her mother's side, on the family farm near Montego Bay, Jamaica. Her mother grew everything the family needed for sustenance, from tangerines, bananas, coconuts, plantains, and avocados to coffee and cocoa beans. Each day, food was freshly picked and prepared. "On Sundays," she recalled, "we made 'rice and peas,' just like every family on the island does." The tasty national dish of Jamaica is made with rice, small dried red beans, a whole fresh coconut, and lots of onions and garlic. After Olive moved to the United States, she so missed her home that she continues to make a big pot of rice and peas each Sunday, giving away portions of it to anyone who comes her way or whom she might be visiting. Doing so, she says, keeps her connected to Jamaican cooking rituals, as well as to the memories of her long-departed mother and her kitchen.

Breakfast comfort

Special breakfast traditions are rarely a lot of work, since they often revolve around just one food. Pancakes, waffles, biscuits, bagels, and fresh muffins seem tailor-made for enjoying in one's pajamas, reading the morning paper. A breakfast ritual can be the perfect antidote to the weekday morning "rush hour" or a special treat on weekends.

✧ Sunday mornings always find Carlie's family (her husband and two school-age sons) around the table with a special breakfast that's not large or elaborate, but different from what they have during the week: "When we were on sabbatical in Cambridge for a year, I made what we call scones, not really English scones, but a kind of cinnamon biscuit, slightly sweet. At home, John makes waffles. We often have some fruit and tea, or coffee and juice. We all look forward to this simple Sunday morning meal—it's a nice way to start the week."

✧ Mary, who has two older school-age children, initiated a ritual that she calls "Thursday pancake day." When Mary was growing up, her mother made pancakes every Friday morning. She has always treasured a vivid recollection of how much fun it was, so she started to do the same for her kids. They, too, love it, but asked that she switch the day to Thursday, their hardest day at school. The pancake ritual gives them comforting sustenance for the day ahead.

✧ Gayil grew up in a small southern town in the 1950s, where hers was the only Jewish family. Bagels and grits for breakfast became the odd yet apt metaphor for preserving cultural identity while trying to fit in. When I asked her if she still eats bagels and grits, she said that this particular combination was strictly of that time and place. Grits are still a top choice for comfort, though. She serves grits and eggs or cheese grits to her family for breakfast on a regular basis.

Breakfast in bed, every day

Every morning, whoever wakes up first (and that's my husband, Rob, 99 percent of the time!) goes downstairs, lets out the dogs and feeds them, then comes back up to bed a few minutes later with a tray (that he built for us) of coffee for him, green tea for me, and toast with almond butter and fruit for us both. We sit in bed, enjoying the view out our bedroom window and read the paper or books and slowly wake up. On mornings when I wake first, I'll bring up bowls of oatmeal with dried fruit and toasted pecans.

On Sunday mornings, we'll often light a fire in our bedroom fireplace, put on some music, get *The New York Times,* and linger in bed even longer than during the week. When our son is home from college, and hasn't stayed up too late the night before, we wake him up and he'll join us at the foot of our sleigh bed (that Rob built, too). We all sip our beverages, eat, read, and chat. Of course, our two dogs end up on the bed, too. We often follow this ritual with a long walk, or snowshoe around our farm in the winter. It's a nice way to start the day!

—Iza Trapani

Our daily bread

Bread is the original comfort food. Few experiences offer more pleasure than the earthy flavors and yeasty aromas of freshly baked bread. Every culture has a characteristic bread, little changed for generations, that's completely ingrained in daily life as well as cultural and religious rituals. Think of Middle Eastern pita bread; Indian *naan, puri,* and *chapatis;* Jewish *challah;* Mexican tortillas.

In the last decade or so, there has been a rediscovery of artisanal bread baking, utilizing traditional European methods, wood-fired ovens, and robust whole grains. Hard on the heels of this phenomenon, however, has come a sign of dissonance—bread is suddenly suspect, a "high carb" hazard. I predict that by the time these words see print, this silly phenomenon will have been put to rest and perhaps even forgotten.

Baking bread at home can be a pleasurable ritual for those who are attracted to its earthy, tactile pleasures. It offers a hands-on way to center oneself, and can be a productive way to enjoy quiet time. Because it engages the senses and requires repetitive movement and some precision, many people who bake bread for pleasure find the process quite meditative.

When Martina received a bread machine from a couple of friends for her fortieth birthday, she thanked them kindly and exchanged it for a slow cooker. For her, the process of baking bread is just as important as the result. Without being involved in the rhythm of kneading, the feel of the dough, and the yeasty scents, she feels she may as well buy bread from the bakery in

Bread makes itself, by your kindness, with your help, with imagination running through you, with dough under hand, you are bread-making itself, which is why breadmaking is so fulfilling and rewarding.

—Edward Espe Brown,
*The Tassajara
Bread Book*

town. Though Martina has two young daughters, her baking ritual helps her claim quiet time that's for herself alone. Since her family almost always spends Friday evenings at home, after dinner, her husband plays board games and reads with the girls. That's their special time with Dad, and Martina's special time to make dough for two large loaves of bread. She takes her time kneading two different batches of dough, finding the process relaxing and meditative; then she sets them in a barely warm oven to rise overnight.

Saturday mornings find Martina up very early. The dough is punched down and shaped into loaves, then she goes out for a run for the duration of the second rising. Once home, the bread is popped into the oven, and the rest of the family wakes to the smell of fresh bread, which is savored throughout the weekend. If any bread is left, it becomes part of Monday night's dinner, served with a soup or stew in her useful slow cooker.

Resources

There are many excellent books on baking bread. Here are two that I like:

Bread Alone: Bold Fresh Loaves from Your Own Hands by Daniel Leader and Judith Blahnick (Morrow Books, 1993)

Breadtime: A Down-to-Earth Cookbook for Bakers and Bread Lovers by Susan Jane Cheney (Ten Speed Press, 1998)

And to inspire kids, here are two books aimed at younger bakers:

Knead it, Punch it, Bake it! The Ultimate Breadmaking Book for Parents and Kids by Judith and Evan Jones (Houghton Mifflin, 1998)

Loaves of Fun: A History of Bread with Activities and Recipes from Around the World by Elizabeth M. and John Harbison (Chicago Review Press, 1997)

Playing in the dough

Baking bread can be a serene, contemplative process. But in my house, it's not. Perhaps it's the ingredients I use: flour, water, yeast . . . oh, yes, and two giggling, flour-covered children.

I began baking bread with my daughter as soon as she could stand on a stool. I thought I was being "educational." Little did I know, I was the one receiving the education. It is fascinating to watch a child's reaction to the bread-baking process. They crinkle their noses at the yeasty smells while stirring the ingredients, marvel at the transformation from liquid to dough. But the *coup de gras* is kneading—the feel of the dough as they bury their hands in it and the taste as their little fingers find their mouths. A total sensory experience!

One of the best things about baking bread is how long it takes. Bread baking is a process, a project. None of the steps are difficult or take very long. In fact, only thirty to forty-five minutes of activity is needed, but that activity is spread over several hours. And it is those hours that make all the difference! During that time, you and your children will have shared wonder and laughter, developed a common sense of purpose and fun, anticipated the magic of transformation, and reveled in a sense of accomplishment.

Bread baking is messy. We clear off and scrub down the dining room table (a better height for my little ones to knead the dough) and keep the vacuum cleaner standing at the ready. My kids and I each have our designated aprons for bread baking. If I forget to put mine on, they are sure to remind me. Somehow, the simple act of wearing aprons gives us a sense of camaraderie and togetherness.

After mixing the ingredients for the dough, then kneading it, it's time to let it rest. My kids seem to really take to the idea of nap time for the dough. We cover the dough carefully with two towels (Hey, two kids, two towels; I've learned not to argue this point.) and set the timer. We shush each other, giggling, out of the kitchen, to let the dough sleep while we clean up a bit. If I time things right, the kids take their naps along with the bread dough and wake early enough to punch it down for the next rise. They are amazed every time at how it grows!

Probably the biggest thrill for all of us is taking the bread out of the oven. As the smells of baking bread waft through the house, the kids congregate in the kitchen, waiting for that magic moment—the dough has become bread! No point in explaining the chemistry of bread baking. They wouldn't believe it anyway. They know it is magic. Heck, I understand the chemistry, and it still looks like magic to me.

—Christine Whittaker Sofge

Part two
A miscellany of family rituals

The family is changing, not disappearing. We have to broaden our understanding of it, look for the new metaphors.

—Mary Catherine Bateson

family reading rituals

Those of us who were called "bookworms" as girls acquire
the more distinctive title of "bibliophile" when we grow up.
How can anyone complain of being bored when libraries and
bookstores beckon with thousands of unread books? I could
live a parallel existence devoted entirely to reading, and I
know many others who feel the same!

Still, I frequently hear busy women bemoan a lack of time,
patience, or both, to read for pleasure. Others wonder how to
inspire their children to develop a greater love for books. No
matter how "educational" certain TV or computer programs
are, none are more nourishing than reading. On the
contrary, with all that visual stimulus right in your face,
the imagination has little chance to take flight, let alone
soar.

Reading is surely a wonderful way to spend time alone.
But if that kind of time eludes you, establishing rituals
of connectedness around books helps ensure that time is
carved out for literary pleasures. Reading rituals involv-
ing family and friends can be just what's needed to
give books their due on an regular basis. These
can be as simple as designating a special
family reading time, or as sophisticated as forming a book group with a
distinct focus (see more on book
groups on page 122). Here,
then, are a miscellany of
reading rituals:

*If I wanted to search for the
truth, I could find it in story.
Story can take us far, far
beyond fact.*

—Madeleine L'Engle

WAR AND
PEACE
Board
Book

Family reading evenings: Maggie, the mother of three school-age children, has created a cozy family reading ritual. Two evenings a week, the TV, computers, and all other electronic devices are turned off, and everyone convenes in the den for an hour or so of silent reading. An avid baker, Maggie nearly always has wholesome goodies on hand for reading nights. In winter, hot cocoa and a warming fire add a final flourish. A family reading night doesn't necessarily need such distinctive touches, though; it can be as basic as everyone piling into the biggest bed in the house to read silently, or aloud to one another. When older kids and teens have reading to do for school, designated family reading time can make assignments seem less of a chore.

Reading at the table: Most of the time, family dinners should be a time for communication and sharing, but some families designate one evening a week when bringing a book to the table is not only allowed, but encouraged. A simple "nursery food" meal makes this a most comforting pairing of activities. Would you like a bowl of tomato soup and a grilled cheese sandwich with that chapter book? It's also worth considering reading aloud to your children while they snack or during weekend lunches, rather than parking them in front of the television. Meg Cox, author of *The Heart of a Family,* fondly recalls her favorite mealtime ritual: Living close enough to walk home for lunch during her elementary school years, she remembers her mother reading *Treasure Island* or the *Oz* books to her and her siblings while they ate their Velveeta sandwiches on white bread.

Family book groups: Here's an appealing, relatively new idea. This kind of book group can include both parents and older kids or teens; it can also include extended family members. It's a fantastic way to connect with grandparents. Teens are especially prone to losing common ground once shared with grandparents; a shared interest in books can span the gap. Some libraries are now promoting the concept of family book groups, as well as hosting them. If you'd like to keep your family book group private, your library might at least be a good resource for reading lists that appeal to a wide range of ages.

Mother-daughter book groups can be fulfilling for preteen and young teenage girls. This is a nifty way to help them get their wings as readers, while providing a constructive way for growing girls and their mothers to stay connected.

Another way to make a family reading group enticing to older kids and teens is to make it a book-and-film club. Find classic books that have been made into films; read the book first, then watch the movie together on video or DVD (served with plenty of popcorn!). A discussion on the differences as well as the merits of book-versus-movie version can be quite spirited and thought provoking. From classic fiction (*Huckleberry Finn*) to contemporary reality (*A Beautiful Mind*) to timeless fantasy (*The Lion, the Witch, and the Wardrobe*), this kind of book group is sure to appeal to budding bibliophiles.

Resources

The Mother-Daughter Book Club: How Ten Busy Mothers and Daughters Came Together to Talk, Laugh and Learn Through Their Love of Reading by Shireen Dodson (Perennial, 1997)

www.kidsreads.com lists and comments on classic books as well as newer ones and provides guidance for family book groups.

www.mcpl.lib.mo.us/readers/movies/book.cfm is the address of a web site called *Based on the Book*, which features an exhaustive list of books made into films.

Reading Aloud

Establishing a read-aloud ritual can be one of
the most gratifying ways to enjoy well-spent
family time. If raising children leaves you with
little energy or patience for personal reading,
take comfort in knowing that reading aloud can
be as nourishing for the reader as it is for the lis-
tener. And literacy experts agree that reading aloud
to your children from an early age helps assure
their becoming avid readers later on. Don't limit
reading aloud to preschoolers—school-age children and sometimes even teens love being read to.
Add whatever embellishments you'd like—a warm
beverage, a specific setting, lots of cuddling—to
ensure a prominent place in your child's memory
for this time-honored ritual.

Revisit heroines you loved as a child: Reading these
books to your own children is a thrill, especially
when you can introduce them to heroines you loved
as a child. Remember Betsy and Tacy, Nancy Drew,
Jo March and the rest of the *Little Women, Rebecca of
Sunnybrook Farm?* Revel in their tales of spunk and
courage while sharing them with your daughters.
There's no reason not to try them out on boys,
too. Few children can resist *Pippi Longstock-
ing, Pollyanna,* or *Anne of Green Gables.*

Which spunky heroine am I?

a. Pollyanna
b. Rebecca of Sunnybrook Farm
c. Anne of Green Gables
d. All of the above

It's never too late for a classic: Discovering classics that somehow passed you by is a delight, too. If you somehow missed *Peter Pan, Bambi, Alice in Wonderland, The Secret Garden,* and others as you grew up, share them with your children. Not merely great children's books, but great books altogether, the rich language of classics, experienced aloud, stimulates your imagination as much as your children's.

Fairy and folk tales, ethnic myths, fables, and legends: These make wondrous read-alouds, and their universal themes can be experienced on many levels. Start with the folk stories from your own cultural background, then move on to those of cultures that interest your family.

Create a magical setting: Jennifer not only established a regular time, but an imaginative setting for reading aloud to her children when they were young. With a simple kit, she constructed a "magic house" that they could all snuggle into. Swathing the little structure with a gauzy, rainbow-hued fabric, Jennifer remembers their shared reading time giving them a great sense of safety and cocooning. The diaphanous quality of the light entering their snug shelter, coupled with their favorite stories, was an experience that truly transported them.

Reading aloud for partners: The read-aloud ritual isn't just for parents and children. Instead of crashing out in front of another sitcom or the late news, consider setting aside a quiet hour to read aloud with your partner. Kate and her late husband did just that. Their selection of read-alouds was eclectic, ranging from popular nonfiction (*All Creatures Great and Small,* by James Herriot) to classic literature (*Les Miserables,* by Victor Hugo); *A Wrinkle in Time,* by Madeleine L'Engle, and *The Phantom Tollbooth,* by Norton Juster, were among their choices in children's literature. They also explored Arthurian legends and arcane biographies. What's best about a read-aloud ritual among partners, according to Kate, is "hearing a great story interpreted by your beloved's voice."

Resources

The Read-Aloud Handbook (5th edition) by Jim Trelease (Penguin USA, 2001) is the definitive volume on this subject. Updated every few years, it makes an inspiring case for reading aloud, and supplies a thorough list of the best read-aloud books for several age groups.

The New York Times' Parent's Guide to the Best Books for Children by Eden Ross Lipson (Three Rivers Press, 2000) is a guide to children's literature from picture books through young adult novels, with special recommendations for books that make good read-alouds.

Once Upon a Heroine: 450 Books for Girls to Love by Alison Cooper-Mullin and Jennifer Marmaduke Coye explores classic and contemporary literature for girls.

Great Books for Girls: More than 600 Recommended Books for Girls Ages 3-14 by Kathleen Odean (Ballantine Books, 2002) lists books for different age groups, featuring strong female characters—fiction and nonfiction.

Great Books for Boys: More than 600 Books for Boys Ages 2–14 by Kathleen Odean (Ballantine Books, 1998) is a companion book to the one above, with a masculine slant.

When you read silently, only the writer performs. When you read aloud, the performance is collaborative.

—Anne Fadiman,
Ex Libris: Confessions of a Common Reader

Sweet dreams: Bedtime rituals for a good night

Families with toddlers and young children know that having solid bedtime rituals is critical for maintaining sanity. To hear my husband tell it, I went overboard with the nightly routine when my sons were young. He may be right, but the trade-off was that bedtime was never stressful and almost always a lot of fun. Snacks on a tray, favorite picture books, and above all, the absurd stories told in the dark ensured that bedtime would be anticipated rather than dreaded.

Bedtime routines and rituals have seen reams of print and are often nothing more exciting than a bath, a snack, and reading aloud or a story, done in a consistent, orderly, and loving fashion. Though such rituals are well covered in parenting literature, I enjoyed the clever tips and stories that came my way, and couldn't imagine leaving this topic out. I'd also argue that in families with toddlers and preschool children, the bedtime ritual is more important as a daily ritual than dinner at the table. When kids go to bed happy, with little resistance, sweet dreams are assured.

✧ Kids adore made-up bedtime stories starring themselves. They can be fairly mundane tales of them taking part in their favorite activities, interacting with family and friends, or being especially good at something. Weaving the events of the day that has just ended into the "story of your day" is a thrill for small children. Recapping the day helps bring order to their many new experiences and sensations—the day's events are "tucked in" along with the child. Of course, kids also love being the central character in an adventure or fantasy tale, if you and your parental imagination are so inclined. One father made his daughters princesses, pirates, and presidents in his nightly stories, having them face and overcome extraordinary hurdles. In stories I told my sons, they interacted with characters from books and movies.

✧ The read-aloud ritual reigns supreme as a bedtime staple in many homes. For ideas on how to make the most of it, see Reading Aloud, page 33.

✧ When older children want to go to bed with their own book, some small ritual of connection can be preserved, like a chat accompanied by warm cocoa or a relaxing back rub.

✧ Many families tell of a favorite bedtime story ritual in which the story always begins the same way, such as "Once there was an elephant and a mouse." Each family member participating adds a sentence, ensuring that the outcome is amazingly different with each telling.

✧ In some families, stuffed animals play a role in the nightly ritual. Sometimes they "talk" to the children about what went on in their rooms while they were out of the house; in other instances, they are set up to patrol the room while the children sleep, keeping them safe from monsters and unpleasant dreams.

✧ If you're not much of a storyteller, start a "Bedtime Q&A" tradition, suggests magicalchildhood.com. creator Alicia Bayer. "When you tuck in your child, designate some time to ask questions about the day or about life in general. You could make it structured, every night asking what was something they learned, what was something good that happened and something bad

I hated to see bedtime rituals end with my children. I remember when my son was about 13, and said two nights in a row that he didn't want to talk that night. The second time I asked, "Shall we leave it that you ask me if you want to talk?" I knew it was over. I found my wife downstairs, and cried.

—William J. Doherty,
The Intentional Family

Pine tree gently sigh
Sing a lullaby
For my baby

Little brooklet flow
Murmur soft and low
For my baby

Breezes come and sing
Let the cradle swing
For my baby

—Chippewa (Native
Americaan) Lullaby

. . . and then you should answer too. Or you can ask different questions of each other every night—everything from what sort of tree do you think you'd be to who do you most admire."

✧ Jennifer and her two children have long enjoyed a tradition of winding down their day by sharing a big platter of nicely arranged fruit served on her king-sized bed. Everyone piles in to eat fruit, chat, and cuddle. Often, even the dog joins in. Jennifer thinks that each day needs to end with lots of cuddling. Having lived in Europe, where more affection is displayed, she feels that Americans need to be more demonstrative.

✧ Some parents sing special songs to lull their kids to sleep (and others use more boisterous or silly songs to get them up in the morning). Deb has always included singing in her daughter's bedtime ritual. A particular song was sung, until such time as another would take its place. Memorable ones included *Sweet Baby James* (James Taylor), *The Man in the Moon* (Mary Chapin Carpenter), and *The Circle Game* (Joni Mitchell).

✧ Before bedtime, do gentle stretches with your children to release tension—yours and theirs. Yoga postures such as Child's Pose are also relaxing, as is lying face up, palms up, visualizing each part of the body, then releasing any tension held there. A number of books on yoga for children are available; see which suits your needs.

✧ Lisa Ross recalled a number of relaxation rituals that her children enjoyed when they were very young. When her son was a baby, her young daughter played a lyre to lull him to sleep. During winter months, she tucked a hot water bottle in with each child to keep them toasty while they heard their bedtime stories. They also play a game called "listen to the silence," during which they listen for a couple of minutes, then relate what they've heard—a passing car, breathing, the rumbling of a tummy.

✧ Visualization can be a creative way to get your children from an active, alert state to a restful one. In a darkened room, talk them through a relaxing scenario—for example, describe to your child in a soothing voice how he or she is walking on a beach, listening to the waves break, watching the wispy clouds in the sky. Once in a while, a dolphin leaps out of the water, and a beautiful shell is picked up and admired.

If we as parents want to pass on our values and raise strong, confident children, we have to be more deliberate about our parenting. Holding family meetings is one of the quickest, easiest ways to improve communication and build character within our families.

—Elaine Hightower and Betsy Riley, *Our Family Meeting Book*

family meeting

"When we were children, families shared mealtimes, leisurely summer evenings on the patio, weekly worship services, and long car trips to grandmother's house," write Elaine Hightower and Betsy Riley in *Our Family Meeting Book*. "Families didn't need meetings because they hashed out mutual concerns around the dinner table. But with both parents working and children participating in more structured activities than ever before, hectic schedules are squeezing out the household rituals which bonded past generations." Apparently, today's families do need meetings. It's a growing trend—structuring a day, time, and agenda to convene as a family and explore issues, arrange schedules, take care of nuts-and-bolts items, and air both appreciation and gripes.

For ten years, Jan, her husband, and son held a family meeting every Sunday. The ritual was sweetened by preceding it with a special brunch. Family meetings followed a pattern than Jan and Steve gleaned from a communication retreat, which created a productive structure to follow. The three of them also coordinated their plans for the week, noting special events or changes in schedule. Jan says that their Sunday brunch-and-meeting ritual was something to count on and an ideal way launch their busy weeks. When their teenage son began sleeping until all hours of the day on Sunday, Jan sensed that this ritual was about to shift. Once their son left for college, the weekly meetings ended by necessity. She misses it, of course, but still enjoys a leisurely Sunday brunch with her husband. Here's a sample schedule to follow for family meetings:

✧ Start out with positives and good news.

✧ Go on to "business"—schedules and activities for the upcoming week, as well as things that need to be done (talk to Tommy's teacher about the math test) or bought (Tara needs sneakers).

✧ Proceed with gripes and debates, but don't allow them to deteriorate into petty arguments.

✧ Explore a topic of mutual interest to everyone, such as: What can we do to help Grandma more often? How can we earn extra money to buy a trampoline? Or pithier issues, such as: What companies should we boycott because they are polluters? What kind of donation should we make to the food bank for Thanksgiving?

✧ End the meeting by making positive resolutions.

Resource

Our Family Meeting Book: Fun and Easy Ways to Manage Time, Build Communication, and Share Responsibility Week by Week by Elaine Hightower and Betsy Riley (Free Spirit Publishing, 2002) is a workbook filled with inspiration and ideas for those who want lots of great ideas for kick-starting a family meeting ritual. Fifty-two sample weekly themes (such as "What Does Our Family Stand For?" —exploring values, and "Taking your chances"— about risk) are suggested to set the tone or spark discussion. The book shows how to use the family meeting to deal with conflict resolution, create family traditions, set goals and plan activities, celebrate accomplishments, and much more.

Tradition is family insurance against outside pressures that threaten to overwhelm our days and weaken our ties to one another. We do not have to invest energy and time deciding what to do. We know what to do. With the weight of permanence and force of habit, tradition demands our attention.

—Susan Abel
Lieberman,
New Traditions

O ONE who has never become acquainted with the annual path of the earth around the sun, there is a series of the most interesting facts which every thoughtful person takes delight in examining.

The earth's axis of daily rotation is tilted about 23½ degrees to the plane of its path of annual motion around the sun, and its axis of rotation always points in the same stellar direction. During winter time in the northern hemisphere the north pole is turned from the sun, permitting the sun to shine more directly or vertically on that part of it south of the equator. But six months later when the earth arrives half way around its path from this point, the north pole is turned toward the sun which shines more vertically on that part of it north of the equator. At points in the earth's annual orbit half way between these two points just mentioned, the sun shines exactly vertically upon the equator.

It is these four positions of the earth just [...] our four seasons of Winter, Summer, [...]

These are [...] modified by [...] reflects muc[...]

Volunteering as a family

Many busy families wish they had more time to volunteer for causes they believe in or to give something back to their communities. But lest you think it's an impossible dream, a recent survey by Youth Service America reports that teen volunteerism is at an all-time high, indicating a strong level of idealism. Community service is often a high school requirement, and in many cases, once teens get a taste of it, they want to do more. That desire can be instilled in children, even from a very early age.

To make volunteering a part of your family life, create a tradition by making it a regularly scheduled event, whether once a month or once a year. The key is finding a cause that stirs everyone's passions.

Lee's family chose a food pantry called the Cooperative Feeding Program to focus on. For many years, they volunteered in tandem, stocking shelves and serving food. They also take part in an annual food drive called the Postal Carrier's Food Drive, taking place each Mother's Day weekend. They help collect and pack tons of food that people have put in their mailboxes. The boxes are then delivered to the Cooperative Feeding Program.

Each of Lee's three children decided to ask guests to their Bar and Bat Mitzvahs to make a donation to the food pantry in lieu of gifts. Her daughter has extended her involvement by preparing small bags filled with treats and small toys for children serviced by the program. She hopes to expand on her endeavors by getting donations from businesses. By focusing on one charity, and staying involved over a number of years, this family has built a tradition of which they can be proud.

If your family can choose but one big event each year to participate in, consider a walkathon. In many communities, charitable organizations sponsor walkathons to raise money for various causes, particularly to raise research money for disease prevention. Another worthy annual event to consider is participating in the cleanup of a public place, especially ecologically sensitive areas. Inquire with environmental organizations in your area.

Jenny Friedman was a freelance writer when her daughters were young. At the time, she felt a great urge to give something back to her community, but wanted to do something that would allow her to have her daughters (then just three years old and six months old) with her. She and a friend, who also had a three-year-old, came up with the idea of delivering meals together to the home bound, through the Meals on Wheels agency. The two friends would pile the kids into one car, pick up the meals, and make about ten deliveries, twice a month. They took turns staying in the car with the baby while the other would take the two three-year-olds to the doors. The little girls would hand the meals to the elderly or home bound, who would invariably be delighted to see them. Even at so tender an age, the girls gained a lot from the experience— they especially loved all the attention, which made them feel quite important!

Jenny and her friend realized that this volunteer work was actually better with their children than it would have been without them; the extra helping of happiness that came with the plate of food made a big difference. This also got her thinking further about the benefits of doing community service as a family. As her family grew (a son came along later), so did her interest in the subject, which culminated in her writing the ultimate guide creating family volunteering traditions—*The Busy Family's Guide to Volunteering.*

"Each time we volunteer," she writes, "we have an opportunity to teach our children that every human being has worth, that we are stewards of this planet, that the world is a better place when we care for others and they care for us." Acknowledging that finding the time to volunteer can be an obstacle for any family, she reminds us that "lessons can be taught, people's lives changed, and small miracles wrought in only minutes or hours."

Jenny Friedman's guide breaks down the resistance and guilt barriers by showing how fun and gratifying volunteering can be when done as a family. A plethora of opportunities in many areas of interest are explored, with specifics on how to get started. There are the more predictable yet worthy venues of volunteerism, including working with the elderly, hungry, and homeless, and supporting the causes of environment and animal welfare. She also suggests avenues that may not immediately come to mind, such as arts, literacy, peace, and social justice organizations. Recently, my older son participated with a high school team in a local spelling bee to raise money and awareness for Literacy Volunteers of America. It was so much fun that he will likely participate again next year, and I, too, have been inspired to participate in future bees with a friend. An annual tradition is born!

The approach of the winter holiday season and their attendant good will can provide a good catalyst for getting into charitable mode. There are so many traditions of giving that you can initiate at this time of year—serving food in a soup kitchen on Thanksgiving, delivering holiday food baskets to the elderly and home bound, participating in toy drives, adopting a low-income family and helping with their holiday needs.

The Points of Light Foundation sponsors two national events that can serve as springboards for starting family volunteering traditions. The first is Make a Difference Day, falling on the fourth Saturday each October. Visit www.makeadifferenceday.com to find and register projects and get ideas based on what others have done. Next, National Family Volunteer Day takes place on the Saturday before each Thanksgiving. This event is "designed to showcase the benefits of families working together, to introduce community service, and encourage those who haven't yet made the commitment to volunteer as a family." It's an ideal way to kick-start a ritual of volunteerism for your family. Visit www.pointsoflight.org to find out more.

Show your kids that it's amazingly easy to make a difference. Cement volunteerism into your family's values by making it a tradition, whether one day a year, or a half day per month, or an hour a week.

Resources

The Busy Family's Guide to Volunteering: Do Good, Have Fun, Make a Difference as a Family by Jenny Lynne Friedman (Robins Lane Press, 2003) is an excellent resource, extensively described in this section.

Doing Good Together (www.doinggoodtogether.org) is a non-profit organization started by Jenny Lynne Friedman to provide "support, encouragement and information to parents who want to engage with their children in community service, charitable giving, and social, environmental and political action."

A Kid's Guide to Service Projects: Over 500 Service Ideas for Young People Who Want to Make a Difference by Barbara Lewis (Free Spirit Press, 1995) is another great book with ideas in dozens of areas of volunteerism.

Catch the Spirit: Teen Volunteers Tell How They Made a Difference by Susan K. Perry, (Scholastic Library Publishing, 2000) is meant to inspire older kids and teens.

The Giving Box: Create a Tradition of Giving with Your Children by Fred Rogers (Running Press, 2000) is a gently inspiring book by the late television personality.

The Difference a Day Makes: 365 Ways to Change Your World in Just 24 Hours by Karen M. Jones (New World Library, 2005) provides a simple way to make a difference each day in areas including ecology, peace, health, child welfare, and much more.

Reclaim your influence and your vital role in a world you can change. You'll discover that the difference a day makes, while significant for the recipients, is greatest for the giver.

—Karen M. Jones,
The Difference a Day Makes

Family rituals in brief

Family Traditions Calendar: What better way to preserve all the special dates and occasions you want to mark than by designating a calendar specifically for family traditions? It need not be anything more elaborate than a medium-sized month-by-month wall calendar; if you use one of these, you can hang it up where it will be visible by all, but you will need to transfer in the dates anew each year. An alternative to this is to use a "Book of Days" type datebook that remains valid from one year to the next. With either format, use the calendar to mark family birthdays, anniversaries, and unique celebrations and activities (such as "Picasso's birthday," "The day we adopted Mittens," or "Our annual camping trip"). Don't use it to mark down dental appointments, soccer practice, one-time events—save those for your appointment calendar. If you use a book of days as your family traditions calendar, you can also use some of the spaces to record favorite memories and events that occurred on specific dates.

Friday night at the home movies: A surprising number of families I spoke with enjoy ordering pizza and watching videos on Friday evenings. While on a yearlong sabbatical in Cambridge, England, my friend Carlie and her family continued their Friday evening pizza tradition (though she had to make the pizza herself to approximate the American version). They found this ritual especially relaxing after a week of school and work in a place where the language was similar, but the culture very different. Other families reported enjoying their pizza picnic-style at home, on an old blanket in the den, while watching their Friday night movie.

On the surface, pizza and videos might hardly qualify as a ritual, though it's amazing how those families who practice it deliberately avoid making other plans on Friday evenings! It's a simple, inexpensive way to recharge the family's collective batteries, and especially relaxing for home cooks who rarely rely on take-out meals.

"Firsts and lasts": Simple rituals make milestones memorable and significant. Ritual expert Barbara Biziou devised a "last day" ritual with her son to mark the last day of school or camp, the final soccer game of the season, and such. For these occasions, she and her son would enjoy a quiet, candlelit pizza dinner, to reflect on what he would miss about the experience.

Creating your own simple ceremonies for acknowledging firsts and lasts helps children recognize the small but significant passages that go into growing up. I think it's wonderful to make a big deal of graduating elementary school and middle school, not just high school and college. We didn't do so for our sons, and I regret it, so we'll really need to do something big when they finish high school! Think of how you can mark the first tooth lost, first period, first report card, last day of summer vacation, last game of the season, receiving a driver's license, and other milestones, with fun, simple ceremonies.

Family game night: Just a generation ago, most family members were actually home, spending time together in the evening. Who needed a ritual for this? For many of today's families, though, spending an evening at home, playing together, can seem like a revolutionary idea. Some families enjoy having a focus for this together time and have designated an evening per week, especially in colder months, for playing classic board games. A variation on this is working on a jigsaw puzzle together while listening to music or radio programs. An ideal game night takes place after dinner and cleanup; Friday night works well, since homework is not an issue and bedtime is more flexible; otherwise, early Sunday evening works well, and is a nice way to end the weekend.

Spending time together as a family playing classic board games may not seem like a big deal. But this activity is a delightful memory-maker and offers opportunities, especially for younger children to learn fair play, exercise patience, follow rules, and win and lose gracefully. Classic board games like the ones you grew up with are not only fun, but build skills and sharpen mental agility.

Building neighborhood connections: Neighborhoods provide a convenient venue for traditions of friendship and connection, and yet they are sadly underused—promises of "Someday, we'll have a block party" usually mean it probably won't happen. In truth, organizing a block party can be as easy as choosing a date and a central location on the street, and putting a flyer in mail-boxes designating a date and location, and asking everyone to bring snacks and games to share. Potlucks, neighborhood yard sales, holidays, games, and sports can all provide focal points for neighborhood traditions. Consider:

✧ An annual yard sale or "swap meet," followed by a block party. Any unsold or unswapped merchandise can then be gathered and donated to a local charity.

✧ A number of families, couples, or individuals meeting for a monthly potluck and game night. In Sandy's neighborhood, four couples rotate among one another's homes for an evening of dessert and Scrabble.

✧ In Anne's neighborhood, one or more of any number of neighborhood women set out for an after-dinner walk. As they pass by the houses of others in this network, more and more women join up as they spot the group passing by their houses. It's a nice way to connect on warm, pleasant evenings, and has turned neighbors into friends.

✧ An outdoor "farewell to summer" gathering at a local pool or park, with a potluck barbecue and conversation for the adults; games and swimming for kids.

✧ A neighborhood open house to view winter holiday season decor and share hot chocolate and cookies (or wine and appetizers) is a splendid way to kick off the holiday season before everyone gets busy with family gatherings and travel.

Sporting traditions: In an era where the majority of families need more physical activity and just plain fresh air, it can be useful as well as fun to build simple rituals and traditions around sports and athletic pursuits. There are numerous forms that this can take, from a weekly family hike, to a seasonal event (a canoe or bicycle trip each spring), to a single big annual event (like the neighborhood softball game and barbecue celebrated on the last day of school by Mary and her neighbors). A shared athletic activity can become a rite of passage event; in a couple of families I know of, Dad treats each child on his or her first ski trip, one-on-one, once they reach a certain age.

Some families complain that team sports take over their lives while their kids are involved in them. While these can undoubtedly be a burden, others have been fortunate enough to be able to add a few little rituals that make school sports feel more inclusive and less obtrusive. Susie's older son was involved in competitive running during high school, and the parents as well as their kids were totally immersed in the experience, making the season an enjoyable community activity. The parents volunteered to do timing at the finish line or work the concession stand.

Other family sporting traditions can include a weekly bowling outing; regular skating or cross-country ski outings in the winter; a yearly camping trip to a favorite destination that includes hiking, climbing, and/or swimming. When spring rolls around, my husband and younger son know it's time to hoist the canoe onto the top of the car and explore local lakes and swamps. What sporting traditions can you incorporate into your family's repertoire?

Share your passions with your children: Whether you have one child or several, a hectic schedule can leave you feeling that any or all are getting short shrift. Of course, there is nothing wrong with simply scheduling a regular date with each child to go out to eat, or go out for ice cream and a walk—anything that allows for interaction.

An even more creative way to use together time is to share those things with your child that you thought you'd have to shelve until they were grown. If you love music, nature, fine cuisine, making pottery, or outdoor adventure, share these passions with your children by creating rituals, as they become age-appropriate. It makes children feel grown-up and very much included to participate in those activities for which you have obvious enthusiasm. One mother of two daughters told me of a regular activity the three shared as the girls grew up that she called "sharing skills." Through the years, they shared "massages, painting, cooking, music, jewelry making, weaving, and a lot more," as she recalled. Not surprisingly, both young women are now in art school.

Part three
Celebrating, commemorating, and preserving memories

Share our similarities, celebrate our differences.

—M. Scott Peck

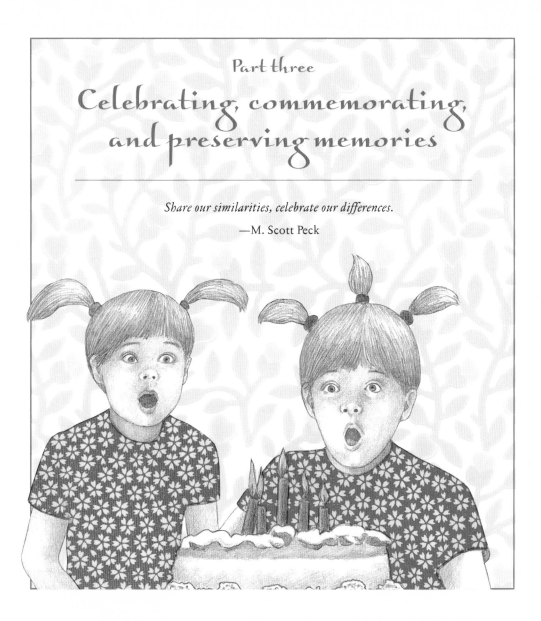

They say it's your birthday

After reaching a certain age, my husband and I grew weary of celebrating our birthdays. When a niece once asked me how old I was, and I answered "thirty-twelve" without missing a beat, I knew I was in trouble. Even the birthday celebrations for our young sons were taking on the forced gaiety of New Year's Eve parties. Planning parties for the boys became a grind, consisting of:

a) choosing a place to gather a bunch of school friends to do an activity for two hours,

b) receiving unneeded gifts,

c) and breathing a sigh of relief when the kids were picked up by their parents.

When I mentioned these "birthday blues" to my friend Stacie, she said that birthdays, in her mind, are a way to celebrate the person and to show appreciation for them. Out of 365 days of the year, one of them should have your name on it. That helped cast a new light on the subject for me. At its best, a birthday can be dedicated to appreciating and honoring the celebrant. Like small, daily rituals of connection, this special celebration need not include fancy or creative elements, but rather those that are meaningful to the birthday boy or girl, whether of the young or grown-up variety.

A meal designed around the birthday person's favorite dishes, or an outing to the restaurant of their choice (my sons love to go out for a special meal in New York City for their birthdays, and for me to make them a chocolate dessert at home); a few words of appreciation spoken around the table after the candles are blown out; gifts that are truly useful and have meaning; a day trip to a much-loved place; a "birthday book" detailing accomplishments of the past year—these and other personal touches can add up to a truly personal and happy birthday.

Birthday letters: Instead of buying store-bought cards, writing birthday letters is a ritual shared by Susan, a single mother, and her three children, ages fourteen, eleven, and nine. Each family member receives a letter from the others on their birthday, ranging from single-page notes to multi-page extravaganzas filled with stickers, drawings, and memorabilia. "I think these letters help the kids to think about what they love about their siblings. They write such amazing letters to each other! In my letters to them, I focus on their accomplishments of the last year, how they've grown, and the steps they've taken toward independence. Getting the letters they write to me is the best part of my birthday. They prove that I'm definitely not taken for granted. If I had to make a quick escape from my house and could only grab one thing, it would be the box of birthday letters from my children."

Mom's birthday letters

My mother wrote a birthday letter to me from the time I was five until I graduated high school. She always included a few photos as well. At first, these birthday letters were thrilling, but by the time I reached high school I found them rather corny and embarrassing. Still, I kept them through the years, and now, long after my mother is gone and my own kids grown, I consider this collection of letters priceless.

I shared my mother's birthday letters with my kids when they were in their early teens, and let me tell you, it was an eye-opener for them! They were able to imagine my childhood more vividly and see all the common threads between themselves and me. I wrote birthday letters to my children from time to time, though far less consistently and thoroughly than my mother did for me. This is something I honestly regret, and that I hope to make up for with my first granddaughter, who was recently born. I look forward to creating birthday letters for her as well as any future grandchildren.

—Andrea Miller

Birthday book: With a little more effort than goes into birthday letters, you can create a yearly "birthday book" for your children. This need not be an entire, extravagant scrapbook; you can keep it simple and take four pieces of sturdy 9- by 12-inch colored paper, folded in half to make an instant sixteen-page booklet. This idea comes from Barbara, who makes a birthday book each year for her daughters, now seven and nine. She pastes in a few recent photos; school information; names and possible photos of current friends; ticket stubs from special events attended; awards; and other memorabilia; listings of likes, dislikes, hobbies, and passions. Not only is the birthday book fun to make as an annual ritual, she says, but each year, all the previous birthday books are brought out, in itself an enjoyable ritual of reminiscence.

Birthday basket: Placing a "birthday basket" on the kitchen table (or other central location) a week or so before a family member's birthday is a simple and fun ritual. In it, the other family members can place cards, informal notes and thoughts, tiny gifts and "I.O.U." coupons that hold promises of special one-on-one times for a movie and dinner night out (promised either by the child or the parent), reprieves from chores, or other favors to be granted. On the day of that person's birthday, wake them up to a birthday breakfast and have them open all the small surprises in their birthday basket.

Simple gifting: *The Simple Living Guide* author Janet Luhrs lists several wonderful, low-impact ideas for birthday gift giving. Asking the guests to bring used toys, books, and sports equipment in good condition to trade can result in a fun "swap meet." Another great idea is to put together a coupon book for the birthday child. Before the party date, ask all the guests to contribute one I.O.U.-type gift. Some examples Luhrs gives are: a sleep over; an afternoon at a favorite bookstore, entitling the birthday child to choose one book to buy; dinner at a friend's house; a weekend date for swimming, horseback riding, etc. Friends as well as family members can contribute to the coupon book. Finally, Luhrs suggests having all the guests bring one of their own toys or books, gift wrapped. The party hosts have a raffle and everyone gets one gift.

Recounting their arrival: For younger children, it's a thrill to hear the story of their arrival into the world as part of the birthday celebration. Build drama into the tale by including details of the anticipation of this wondrous event! Finally, embellish the story by pulling out the first photo taken of them, the certificate that bears their tiny footprint, their tiny nursery cap, and any other memorabilia you have to share.

"Birthday dates" with the kids: When one of my nephews was about eight years old, he decided to take my sister-in-law, Anne, out for a birthday breakfast. With plenty of choices at hand, he nevertheless chose a truck stop diner, where every meal cost $1.39. "Mom," he said as he waved his hand expansively toward the menu, "order anything you want." And so began a "birthday breakfast" tradition that lasted for some years. Anne still prefers a gift of one-on-one time from her now-grown sons for her birthday. For some years now, she and each son try to have a special date around the time of her birthday. It's usually something simple, like a special breakfast, dinner and/or a movie, but it's far more meaningful to her than receiving a purchased gift. Kids can be unsure what to buy for their parents' birthday (and often have limited means), so expressing a preference for shared time can be a blessing for the giver and receiver alike. Having kids make a standing date to spend with grandparents on their birthdays is an equally thoughtful and gratifying ritual.

Seasonal connections: Link your own cyclic rhythms and the earth's. Your birthday is a perfect occasion to celebrate in a meaningful way that reflects the season of your birth. I have a favorite ritual for my mid-spring birthday, when our region is beginning to blossom, and the days grow longer and warmer. My family and I go to a beautiful land preserve that's both serene and stunningly beautiful. We hike to an observation tower called Skytop, from which we can see five states on a clear day; we canoe or paddle boat on a small jewel of a lake; we scramble through rock formations; and we stop for a picnic at Lily Pond, which teems with new life—tadpoles, baby turtles, and fish. This yearly ritual helps me begin another chapter of my life with a renewed sense of hope and the promise of adventure.

The big giveaway: Prior to birthdays (as well as major holidays), it's good to convey to children the importance of making space and sharing what is outgrown or no longer needed. Both of Marina's children's birthdays are in mid-November, so she tries to make this an annual ritual that's fun, and promotes a sense of generosity. Three or more boxes are prepared, marked "Women's shelter," "For friends," and "Thrift shop." She lets the girls give items to friends, and when they were old enough, she began taking them to personally deliver clothes, toys, and books to a local shelter so they could see their giving in action.

"New Privilege, New Responsibility": Gertrud Mueller Nelson, author of *To Dance with God: Family Ritual and Celebration,* writes of a ritual that is also a mini rite of passage for each year. On their birthdays, she gave her children two envelopes: One was marked "New Privilege" and the other, "New Re-

sponsibility." A child turning six might be given the privilege of staying up an extra half hour at night, and the responsibility of feeding the dog its dinner. This ritual, writes the author, "gave them a sense of importance and made them feel grown up."

Document the day: Many of us get lax about photographing and videotaping our kids on a regular basis; make sure to use the occasion of their birthday to do so. You can use a mini photo album for each year, date it, and store in a photo box. Date and store each videotape in a specially designated "birthday box." The fun part is revisiting these memories in subsequent years, and this, in fact, can become part of each year's birthday ritual.

A day off for all

When I was growing up, the birthday child was pampered for an entire week, during which we could do whatever we wanted—including eating ice cream for breakfast, not doing our chores—all nice distractions while anticipating our birthday party. Now, my family has embellished the tradition by adding a day off for the entire family on each person's birthday. Dad doesn't go to work and we take a family day trip to the zoo, a museum, or wherever the birthday person wants to go. Even the birthdays of the adults in our family are celebrated with a special day off.

—Sylvia Diaz

Birthday customs, ancient and modern

Your children might enjoy knowing the meaning behind some of our deeply ingrained birthday customs, such as why we have birthday cake and blow out candles. Similarly, learning about birthday customs from around the world, and perhaps incorporating some of them into our own celebrations, can add an offbeat spark that keep festivities from becoming rote.

✧ It's commonly accepted that many modern birthday customs originated in 19th-century Germany, particularly the traditions of parties, cakes, and blowing out candles. Candle making was quite an art in Germany, and this is believed to be the place where setting small candles on cakes got started. Blowing out all candles at once was thought to bring good luck, which later came to symbolize having one's wishes granted.

✧ The cake-and-candles custom may have had even earlier roots: Legend has it that the ancient Greeks once took round cakes, to represent the full moon, to the temple of the goddess of the moon, Artemis. Candles were put on the cake to represent the glowing moon.

✧ It's not uncommon to find American children taking aim at piñatas at birthday parties. This custom originated in Mexico, of course. In this three-hundred-year-old tradition, piñatas are filled with candies and treats shaped as animals or stars.

✧ In Japan, all birthdays were once celebrated on January 1, no matter when the person's actual birth date. It was a national day of birthdays! Today, most Japanese people celebrate their birthday on the true date on which they were born. One modern custom is for the birthday person to wear an entirely new set of clothes for the occasion.

✧ In China, a common birthday custom is to invite relatives and friends to lunch and serve long noodles to symbolize a long life for the child.

✧ In the British Isles, one charming tradition was serving "fortune telling cake" to the birthday person. Small symbolic objects were baked into the birthday cake. Finding a coin in one's piece of cake, for example, foretold future riches.

✧ In India, it was customary for the birthday child to wear particularly brightly colored clothing and to distribute chocolates to classmates.

✧ In Israel, the birthday child sits in a chair. His or her family and friends raise and lower the child in the chair, the number of "raises" corresponding with the child's age, plus one more for good luck.

✧ Finally, what can you do for that rare child who doesn't care for cake? Do what has long been done in Russia and make a birthday pie, with a greeting carved into the crust.

Resources

Happy Birthday, Everywhere! by Arlene Erlbach (Millbrook Press, 1998) is filled with ideas on customs, games, and recipes for children's birthdays from around the globe.

The Ultimate Birthday Party Book: 50 Complete and Creative Themes to Make Your Kid's Special Day Fantastic! by Susan Baltrus (Chariot Victor Publishing, 2002) offers fun thematic ideas for out-of-the-ordinary birthdays.

The Penny Whistle Birthday Party Book by Meredith Brokaw and Annie Gilbar (Fireside Books, 1992) explores a myriad of ideas for fun birthday parties at home.

Creating unique family celebrations

The spirit craves celebration through occasions set apart from the ordinary. If the celebratory rites you grew up with no longer resonate, or if you simply wish to make them more surprising and less rote, gather with your family, turn on the creative juices, and explore how you can create celebrations that are meaningful to all of you. This section will concern itself more with smaller and unique celebrations rather than the traditional holidays. However, whether or not you celebrate traditional holidays (and I'm in no way suggesting that you abandon your traditions), why not think of marking special occasions, large or small, personal or universal, in ways that are unique to your family? You might also consider giving existing traditions a fresh spin that suits the needs and beliefs of your family. For example:

✧ Amanda's favorite holiday had always been Thanksgiving, but after her divorce and parents' deaths, the day felt more depressing than festive. With two preteens at home, she still wanted to so something meaningful as well as fun. Though the kids fought it tooth and nail at first, Amanda decided that the three of them should volunteer at a local soup kitchen. They helped serve the Thanksgiving meal around noon, leaving much of the rest of the day to do something for themselves. Amanda also organized a potluck dinner for others whose families lived far away or who, for various reasons, had no plans for Thanksgiving. Years later, Amanda still enjoys this rewarding recasting of her favorite holiday. Her son and daughter are now in college, and occasionally spend Thanksgiving break with their father or a friend, but their mom's Thanksgiving tradition—especially the volunteering—rates highest with them.

✧ Cynthia and her husband each have several siblings, so Christmas gift-buying had become daunting as their families grew. Though they still buy gifts for all the nieces and nephews, the adults decided that they would make small donations in one another's name to that person's favorite charity.

✧ Terry's family no longer ascribes to the religious aspects of Passover, but didn't want to "do nothing," as she puts it, on this important Jewish holiday. "I still wanted us to feel connected to Jews around the world." Her family and guests still have a festive meal on the first night of

Passover. However, instead of the traditional Seder, they serve foods that celebrate spring, and read passages of their choosing on the meaning of freedom, a central theme of this holiday.

✧ Kwanzaa is a prime example of how holiday hoopla can be transformed into meaningful ceremony. A modern holiday with ancient roots, it was first celebrated in 1966 after being developed by Dr. Maulana Karenga (then chair of the department of Black Studies at California State University, Long Beach), to underscore the need to preserve African American culture. Though celebrated from December 26 through January 1, Kwanzaa is not religious and avoids commercial trappings, instead focusing on family, community, and culture. Dr. Karenga drew its principles, and its name, from the first harvest celebrations of Africa. Celebrating the cultures of a number of African communities, it is now practiced by millions of Africans of all faiths and languages throughout the world! One man's creation of a celebration now so beloved by families around the globe can surely inspire individual families to design festive rituals with special meaning for themselves.

It's for each family to decide which holidays traditional to their own cultural background to celebrate, to what extent, and with what unique elements. Holidays and celebrations can be the most daunting for those in single-parent families and mixed-tradition partnerships, but these circumstances can also allow for the most creativity. Consult the resources at the end of this section for many excellent ideas.

Our homes need revelry as much as we do. Few things enliven a residence as thoroughly as giving it a reputation for celebration. Every holiday marked there, every congratulatory dinner, every open house honoring visitors from far away—these add up to make your house or apartment a place that radiates warmth, hospitality, and memories by the roomful.

—Victoria Moran,
Shelter for the Spirit

"Wonderment"

My daughter, Lexi, was always asking us why we don't celebrate Christmas or Hanukkah. Neither my husband, Jamie, nor I "vibed" with either holiday. So we came up with our own holiday, which we call Wonderment. The first Saturday of each New Year, we invite all our friends and family to come celebrate the wonder of just being alive.

To honor our connection to each other and to the universe, we ask our guests to bring two things. First, a trinket, a charm, or a small token attached to a string that we can hang from our "Wonderthing." The Wonderthing (the base is a huge lamp with four arms) is a work in progress, evolving into a symbol of our connection to each other. Second, we request that each person bring a unique candle that we place on the mantle of our fireplace.

We hope that this holiday gives us, and everyone we love, a special opportunity to be wonderful with our selves and with each other. We ask that every person bring a thought to share on what aspect of life fills his or her heart with wonder and the joy of being here on planet earth. Each person's candle is lit as we in turn share our thoughts on what Wonderment means to us. After our ceremony, we eat lots of food, dance, have a drumming circle, and mingle with people of all ages, diverse ethnic backgrounds, and religious beliefs. Kids and adults alike leave our house feeling loved and appreciated.

This year we celebrated our third Wonderment. And this year, like the two before it, we received call after call telling us how meaningful and fulfilling it was to share in our holiday. It feels good to have co-created a day each year to celebrate the wonder of just being.

—Alison Greenberg

Borrow from other cultures: If there is a culture that fascinates you or any members of your family, borrow from it to create festive celebrations. New Year celebrations, harvest festivals, seasonal and celestial rites, and other nondenominational holidays can give your family a fresh, exciting perspective and teach children to appreciate cultures other than their own. Even a superficial nod to the celebratory rituals of global cultures helps foster tolerance in a world growing ever smaller. Acknowledging *Cinco de Mayo* (Mexican Independence Day), *Diwali* (the Hindu Festival of Lights), or the Chinese New Year, is cultural education disguised as fun. There are plenty of books on these subjects geared to kids, and lots of information on the internet.

Chinese culture has fascinated my younger son ever since he studied it in second grade. Thanks to him, we've been celebrating the Chinese New Year for some years. At the start of this two-week festival, he decorates our kitchen with his dragon collection and creates a centerpiece with dragons, candles, oranges, and the customary coin-filled red envelopes. On the first night, we enjoy a homemade Chinese meal. One year, we attended a festive celebration hosted by the local Chinese community, another, we attended a performance of the Beijing acrobats. Each year, we add a little something to the celebration; it has become a tradition that adds shimmer to the dismal days of February.

Similarly, multi-ethnic rituals can be woven into standard holidays to make them a richer experience. Take the New Year celebration, for instance. Many of us find this an occasion of forced gaiety, devoid of either meaning or real fun. Instead of watching the televised ball drop on Times Square, consider some traditions from around the world to add spark to family New Year celebrations. Here are a few customs from cultures that celebrate the New Year on January 1, so we can catch their spirit:

✧ In Finland, the New Year is really played up, as it comes at the darkest time of year, when daylight is scarce indeed. A light meal, sauna, and fireworks are customary. The Finns also play games to foretell the future on New Year's Eve. This traditionally has taken the form of a melted piece of tin in a container of water—something a bit arcane for us non-Finns. Try a ready-made form of divination, such as tarot cards or the *I Ching*. Explore these and other divination tools at a New Age shop as part of the fun.

✧ Numerous traditions are associated with the Japanese New Year. Friends and family forgive one another for any disagreements, so that everyone can start the new year fresh. On December 31, bells or gongs are rung 108 times to dispel 108 troubles, followed by gales of laughter, in the belief that laughing drives away troubles and bad spirits. With the spirit of forgiveness, and with all troubles driven away, a day of celebration follows.

✧ Eat twelve grapes at the stroke of midnight, as is the custom in Spain. Each grape, representing one month of the year, is eaten for every stroke of the clock. This custom is believed to bring good luck in the new year.

✧ Black-eyed peas are considered a good-luck food in the American Deep South and are traditionally eaten on New Year's Day. Sometimes, a few coins are mixed into the dish, and finding a coin in your helping brings good luck. Cook up a big batch of Hoppin' John (black-eyed peas with rice—you'll find recipes for this simple dish in many southern cookbooks), toss in a few quarters, forewarn your company, and enjoy!

Celebrate your heroes and heroines: Celebrating the birthdays of great thinkers, authors, and leaders is a fantastic way to teach kids about cultural icons. If you admire Gandhi, for example, commemorating his birthday is an opportunity to honor his wisdom and compassion. Is there an author, poet, or musician that your family particularly admires? For youngsters, celebrating the birthdays of classic authors can be a rollicking good time. Imagine a "Mad Hatter's tea party" for Lewis Carroll, a picnic highlighting honey-flavored goodies for Winnie-the-Pooh creator A.A. Milne, and for Dr. Seuss—well, anything goes.

Happy Birthday, Mozart

One of our best celebrations was an impromptu birthday party for Mozart. Rachael was eight and quite taken with the thought of someone her age composing, so on the draggy winter afternoon—January 27, to be exact—we played Mozart tapes and baked a sheet cake. There was some half-used cake decorating gel left over from the birthday of someone still living, so we used it to regale Wolfgang's cake in quarter notes and sharps and flats. Then we rented the film *Amadeus*. A week later I overheard Rachael asking one of her friends what he had done for Mozart's birthday. Holidays are in the eye of the beholder. We now do Mozart's birthday every year.

—Victoria Moran,
Shelter for the Spirit

Celebrate smaller holidays: If you don't wish to create your own celebrations "from scratch," take cues from what is already on the calendar, which offers ample opportunities for small celebrations throughout the year. Explore how you can tailor them to your family's liking. Groundhog Day, for instance, coming at one of the year's dreariest times, can be an occasion to create traditions for coaxing spring (planting seedlings in pots, bringing in branches of flowering shrubs to force indoors). Or, watch the wonderful movie of the same name accompanied by a meal consisting of your family's favorite cold-weather comfort foods—served on a picnic blanket on the floor. Here's a good example of how just one month offers lots of small occasions to celebrate. Far from being the proverbial "cruelest month," April offers ample opportunities beyond the major holidays of Easter and Passover:

✧ April is National Poetry Month. Have everyone bring a favorite poem to share at the dinner table once a week, or make it a month to read poetry at bedtime instead of stories.

✧ April Fool's Day can be celebrated with humor (rather than playing pranks). Read favorite humor books aloud, and watch classic comedies—the Marx Brothers, Charlie Chaplin, Mel Brooks, Woody Allen.

✧ Earth Day falls on April 22, and many communities offer an abundance of activities for families. You can participate in those, or fashion your own earth-friendly tradition, such as cleanup of a favorite park or shore path. Earth Day Network (www.earthday.net) is a site devoted to celebrating Earth Day on April 22 and throughout the year.

✧ Arbor Day, which usually falls on the last Friday in April, can inspire your family to create a yearly tree-planting ceremony. National Arbor Day Foundation (www.arborday.org): For a nominal membership fee, this organization will mail you ten young trees to plant that are just right for your part of the country, with instructions and tips for maintenance.

The turning of the seasons also offers many opportunities for small rites of celebration. If you haven't yet had your fill after April's celebrations, May starts off with May Day—or if you prefer, the pagan Beltane. For seasonal ideas, see Seasonal rites, page 79.

Resources

The Book of New Family Traditions: How to Create Great Rituals for Holidays and Everyday by Meg Cox (Running Press, 2003) has lots of ideas for making traditional and smaller holidays more fun, especially for younger children.

New Traditions: Redefining Celebrations for Today's Family by Susan Abel Lieberman (Farrar Straus Giroux, 1991) is also an excellent book on giving fresh life to customary holidays and traditional celebrations (like anniversaries, Mother's Day, and such). The author doesn't shy away from addressing issues like divorce and unconventional families in this context.

Kids Around the World Celebrate!: The Best Feasts and Festivals from Many Lands by Lynda Jones (Wiley, 1999) is a book of lore and recipes for multicultural holidays.

The Official Kwanzaa Web Site (www.officialkwanzaawebsite. org) was created by its originator, Dr. Maulana Karenga. And most any library system has numerous books on Kwanzaa aimed at young readers, with lore, crafts, activities, and recipes.

When old traditions lose their vitality or cease to serve, we should unravel them and mix old threads with new to weave new family traditions that give us shared experiences and togetherness.

—Susan Abel Lieberman, *New Traditions*

Preserving family memories

Taking regular pictures and videotapes of your children and family adventures, then organizing them in some chronological fashion is admirable (and more than most parents manage to do!). Keeping scrapbooks and boxes of memorabilia is no small feat, either, but pulling them out from time to time to reminisce over is a priceless pleasure. Though it may often seem daunting, no one regrets the investment of time put into preserving family photos and memorabilia, no matter what shape the endeavor takes. For these purposes, though, let's look at a few ways to turn the process of preserving family memories into fun traditions.

Take a photo at the same time and place each year: Marcia and her husband planted a tree to honor the birth of each of their three children, reflecting an ancient custom shared by many cultures. From the time each child could stand, he or she was photographed on their birthday, next to their special tree. The photos serve a poignant reminder of the fleeting nature of childhood, yet at the same time they are anchors, rooting each child in time and place.

From the time they were eight and ten years old, Janice and Becky's father has taken their photo together on a bench in front of their family's lake cottage. The photo has always been taken on or around the Fourth of July. Thirty years later, the sisters feel fortunate that their father is still in good health and willing to take their tandem photo on that same bench any time they happen to visit their parents together during the summer.

Stacie feels that the annual family reunion she hosts each summer (see Keep family stories alive with reunions, following) would not be complete without a photograph of the entire clan of aunts, uncles, siblings, and cousins. To extend the pleasure of this same-time, same place ritual, you can create a chronological display of the photos somewhere in your home.

Create a time capsule: Here's an easy, engaging activity, ideal for doing during the lull between the winter holidays and New Year's Day, when the old year is winding down (though any time you find more convenient is fine). It takes but a few fun-filled hours, and creates a concrete link to your family's history as well as the culture at large, for many years to come. Choose a sturdy plastic storage container, the size of a shoe box, or perhaps a bit larger. Collect some or all of the following to place inside it:

✧ The front section of an issue of the daily newspaper, enclosed in sturdy plastic wrapping

✧ A weekly newsmagazine

✧ Extra or duplicate family photos from the past year (those that aren't needed for albums)

✧ Any ephemera you may have about the past year's popular books and movies (such as a best-seller list or top 10 movie lists), and other cultural phenomena (clip these from magazines, and/or include any programs or tickets saved from events your family has attended)

✧ Maps and brochures from the past year's family trips

✧ Memorabilia about home, garden, and companion animals

✧ Photocopies of awards from school and camp

Which do you think your kids will remember most? The pricey family vacation to Disney World, or the tea with toast and jelly you always made them when they were sick? Surprise—it's the tea and toast, or rather, the small, everyday routines that endure. . . . Even the simplest rituals make children (and parents) feel that they're part of a unit, which is key to imbuing kids with a sense of security.

—Elaine Galinsky,
Work and Families
Institute

You may think of other personal and cultural items you might like to place in your family's time capsule in addition to those listed above. Just make sure not to use items you'll need or want any time soon, like original awards and report cards, or the last remaining photo of your departed cat. Finally, have everyone sit down and think of favorite books, movies, concerts, and plays, memorable outings and restaurant meals, and other events and accomplishments from the year just past. Have a designated list-maker note all these items (or have everyone make their own list), including any special anecdotes.

Seal the box and affix a note on it: "Do not open until . . ." whatever date is mutually agreed upon. For younger children, even a year seems like a long time, but older children might agree to a waiting period of two to five years. Put the box in a safe spot. You need not bury it in the ground—stashing your time capsule in an attic or out-of-the-way closet is sufficient. If you start this tradition when your children are young, there will be a box to open each year and reminisce over, as you and your family put together the next time capsule.

Keep family stories alive with reunions: After her mother premature death, Stacie's aunts (her mother's sisters) felt a need to stay connected, and started to host yearly family reunions. After a few years, the aunts asked Stacie to hold the next reunion. Since she lives a few hours from where most of the family members live, she was afraid that no one would show up. On the contrary, it was so well attended and so thoroughly enjoyed that Stacie has taken on the permanent task of hosting the reunions, and each year, the number of family members attending has grown. Stacie uses the reunion as a target date and incentive to get things spruced up and fixed around the house and garden; she noted that in a family that has suffered from rifts, the reunion helps heal estrangements.

Over the years, the extended family has established food and activity rituals that make things flow easily throughout this very intensive time together. Sports, skits, barbecues, Irish dance, and a bonfire are among the highlights; but no reunion would be the same without the usual family stories being told, enjoyed, and most important, kept alive.

The family reunion is a subject—indeed, a book—in and of itself. There is copious information on how to plan and host them, as well as various themes and approaches, at your fingertips on the internet. If the idea of reunions seems intriguing, yet daunting, there are many ways to "work up" to them, and they don't necessarily have to involve every living relative you have in the world. You can focus on a certain group of cousins, or on a geographic area where a good number of relatives are clustered. To get started, try sending an "intention letter" or e-mail, to feel out who might be interested in participating in and helping to organize such an event.

Adoption day traditions: Families with adopted children often find simple yet sustaining ways to revisit "the day we got you." Lisa Newman and her husband Dan show each of their daughters, adopted from China, the video taken on the day their adoption became official. They refer to each girl's adoption day as their "anniversary." The girls absolutely love watching the video of Lisa and Dan receiving them as babies; watching the video spurs the retelling of stories and memories of each adoption. This simple ritual is rich enough, says Lisa, without the giving of gifts or a meal, as is customary at birthdays.

family history on file

I'm the keeper of family history, so I wanted to share some of the things I know with everyone else. A few years ago, I went through old calendars, journals, and photo albums and collected significant dates and events. Some were family milestones, like the day we moved into a new house, or when a cousin got married. Others were just moments I wanted to remember—losing a first tooth, or a particularly fun winter day. I took index cards and wrote an event and its year on an index card for that date. Now, every so often, we look at the card for that day's date and talk about what happened in our family on that date. I've also used them to write notes for lunch boxes ("Today was the day you started walking back in 1993"). We often add new events to the cards.

—Reed Mangels

Help your children grow a family tree: Having your children work on creating a family tree at designated family gatherings such as yearly reunions, Thanksgiving, or a regularly held extended family dinner can be a richly rewarding ritual, and another good way to keep family stories alive. Make sure that kids understand that putting a family tree together can be a somewhat lengthy process, rewarded by an understanding of the family's roots and stories. At gatherings, kids can "interview" relatives and gather the following information:

✧ Birth date and place

✧ Date and place of marriage

✧ Ancestral information from older relatives on those who are departed, such as birthplace and date, date of death, where they grew up, and where they are buried

✧ Names, birth and death dates, where they were from, when they married, names of offspring

Many genealogical web sites are available; some are helpful, while others are only there for profit. If your kids want to use web-based information, make sure to investigate sites to help them determine whether they are legitimate and useful. Not surprisingly, software to aid in creating family genealogies is available, and you might want to help your kids decide if they'd like to take a technical route or a more hands-on approach.

How elaborate to make the family tree should be decided upon in advance. It can be as simple as a big pedigree chart on poster board showing names, dates, marriages, and off-spring. Or it can be done as a scrapbook or binder, including pages or pockets for written histories, or family stories recorded on audiocassette. Encourage your kids to capture family stories, as the tradition of keeping them alive orally is certainly on the wane. Hearing about childhoods past is always fascinating for kids; when they hear the old saw about how grandpa walked five miles to school in blinding snow-storms, they are more likely to savor the tale than roll their eyes if they are recording it for posterity.

Photos can also be included in a scrapbook-style family tree. Your kids can ask their aunts, uncles, and grandparents to donate pictures that they are willing to spare for the project, and affix them on appropriate pages. Current pictures that they themselves take can be included as well. If the process of putting together a family tree of any sort starts to outweigh the outcome or reward, consider creating a "family memory box" at a regularly attended event, such as Thanksgiving or the winter holidays, where everyone brings an item or two (dated photos, letters, birth certificates, etc.—photocopies are preferable). The memory box can be "visited" and added to on each of these occasions. It may not be as formal as a family tree or memory album, but is still a simple and rewarding way to preserve family history and stories.

Honoring the departed

In most modern cultures, there are rituals for burying departed loved ones, but few for honoring their memories. Yet rites for honoring ancestors and commemorating the departed are intrinsic to more traditional cultures all over the world. Mexico's Day of the Dead is one example. An elaborate yearly tradition, this joyous celebration encourages viewing death as part of the cycle of changes, not something frightening. Festivities include sugar sculptures of skulls and bones, special breads and other delicious ceremonial foods, colorful decorations, and candlelit midnight marches to graveyards.

Samhain was the Celtic predecessor of today's Halloween, and has much in common with Mexican Day of the Dead. It was a day to celebrate the dead with food, drink, magic, and divination. Cait Johnson, in *Witch in the Kitchen,* writes of Samhain, "Today is the perfect day to set the table with those old plates or glasses that were left to you by your grandmother, your aunt, or your mother. . . . Set an extra place for anyone who died in the past year, or for a special relative or friend. Tell loving stories about them at dinner."

Asian and African cultures have long held cherished rituals for honoring ancestors, who are believed to remain an integral presence in the family. The Korean New Year, for example, also serves as a day for honoring ancestors and strengthening family connections. A central rite of the day honors the past four generations of ancestors.

In other parts of Asia, a special date is set aside as Respect for Ancestors Day. The day begins by leaving offerings of beautifully prepared foods and flowers at grave sites, and ends with a festive meal eaten at home, marking both a tribute to, and separation from the departed.

To the memory of Aunt Sue — Who always had a smile on her face, and who made the best cherry pie. You will always have a place in our hearts.

These ancestor-honoring rituals might be more readily admired than envied outside their cultures. Still, there are many simple ways we can commemorate loved ones once they've passed on.

Ancestor feast: Some families practice a symbolic ritual of remembrance to honor the departed on the anniversary of their birth or death. They set an extra plate at the table, complete with food, lit by a candle, and surrounded by several photos of the departed. Serve that person's favorite dishes, their signature recipes, or foods that reflect their cultural heritage. What were some of the special dishes they made that left a lasting impression on you? Have your children help in selecting and preparing foods for this commemoration. The flavors and aromas associated with a relative's favorite foods are a concrete way to bring memories alive. And if not an entire meal, baking or cooking something just like Mom, Dad, or Grandma did can be just as effective a way to pass something of that person along to your own children.

Memorial altar: Consider creating a special altar on the person's birthday, with flowers, photos, and other memorabilia, as is done in some Eastern cultures. Place a special plate of food as an offering, perhaps special foods symbolizing those enjoyed by the person being honored. Tell stories and share memories about the departed. If one of your or your partner's parents or grandparents is being honored, your children may especially enjoy finding out more about their ethnic backgrounds. Prepare a meal reflecting their cultural background; look at maps of the region, or a globe, to locate where they were born and grew up.

I know a woman who sets out a picture of her friends and relations who have died. She lights a candle next to each picture and thinks about them. It might be a good idea to take out some few heirlooms or the family photo album and go through the pictures of those who have died and have a story-telling session that keeps alive the legends that surround these persons.

—Gertrud Mueller Nelson, *To Dance with God*

At Samhain we set a place
at our table for the people
we love who have died and
we cook a dish or two that
were their special favorites.
We usually put a small
portion of every food and
drink that we serve for
Samhain on a special plate
and in a special cup, which
are set on the table at the
empty place—the Ancestor
Seat. . . . Pick a dish than
reflects who you are, the
culmination of countless
generations, and give some
thought to the amazing
chain, reaching back beyond
memory, of life continuing
itself.

—Cait Johnson,
Witch in the Kitchen

"Ancestral vessel": In some societies, vase-like containers were once fashioned to hold small worldly belongings of the departed. If you have small items that belonged to a departed loved one, consider making or purchasing a modern version of a "reliquary vessel." This can be a decorative box and used for storing small keepsakes that belonged to that person, such as watches and other jewelry, passports, coins, medals, awards, or other items that may have been part of their personal collection, plus some photos of or belonging to them. Each year, on the anniversary of this person's birth or death, the container can be taken from its special place. The objects and photos can be laid out to admire, and reminisce over, keeping alive the unique story of the individual's life.

Create an annual memorial tradition: Susie's brother died at age forty-five from non-Hodgkin's lymphoma. He was a professional photographer by trade. Ken's buddies from his college newspaper days came up with the idea of creating an endowment (funded by former classmates) for an annual photo contest open to anyone presently on the newspaper's staff. Susie helps judge the submissions each year, and the winner receives a $500 scholarship in Ken's name. It has become an annual tradition that continues to heal family and friends of Ken and to honor him by encouraging others to excel at what was his personal passion.

Plant a memory garden: Here's a lovely and lasting tribute. Plant a small garden in honor of the departed. Consider having a small tree, such as a Japanese maple or weeping cherry, as the centerpiece. Designate an annual ritual of adding something to the garden in the late spring or early summer of each year. If space allows, place a bench near this garden for sitting, meditating, and remembering.

Honor what was unique about your loved ones: Commemorate the individual by celebrating their interests and hobbies. Maybe your dad loved baseball. Take his memory out to the ball game on his birthday. Was Aunt Sue famous for her baking? Recreate her signature recipe. Perhaps Grandma was an activist. Volunteer for or contribute to her favorite cause on her birth date.

Sparkling memories

My husband's Aunt Jane, who was Armenian, was quite a sparkly woman. She wore sparkly clothes, handbags, shoes, and scarves. If the item didn't come with sparkle, she'd add sparkle to it. Sequins, beads, jewels—anything than reflected light. She even added sparkle to the floral print of her wallpaper and the seams of her parquet floors. She passed away a few years ago and is missed by all of us. My mother-in-law decided that in honor of her sister, we all needed to do something to remember Aunt Jane.

Each year, on the anniversary of Aunt Jane's birthday, all of us "girls" pile in the car and go down to Patterson, New Jersey, where there is a Middle Eastern community. Each of us gets a bangle bracelet, reflecting the Armenian custom in which, starting at age thirteen, Armenian girls get a bangle from their mother as a gift. And so, we each get ourselves a gift of a sparkly bangle—it has to be sparkly!— to remember and commemorate Aunt Jane.

—Gina Luna Maserjian

Part four
Seasonal rites

*Those who contemplate the beauty of the earth find reserves of strength that will
endure as long as life lasts. There is symbolic as well as actual beauty in the migra-
tion of birds, the ebb and flow of the tides, the folded bud ready for the spring. There
is something infinitely healing in the repeated refrains of nature—the assurance that
dawn comes after night, and spring after the winter.*

—Rachel Carson, *The Sense of Wonder*

*When we honor the an-
nual cycles of sprouting,
growth, fruiting, decaying,
and sprouting again, we
give ourselves the gift of
serenity. There is some-
thing deeply satisfying
and reassuring about those
cycles, a promise of birth
and renewal while honor-
ing the processes of death
and decay. By consciously
aligning ourselves with the
pattern we honor our own
processes—and we make a
deep and powerful connec-
tion with our planet.*

—Cait Johnson and
   Maura D. Shaw,
   *Celebrating the
   Great Mother*

When my younger son was in kindergarten, his class made a construction paper graph to determine which season was the kids' favorite. With less than a handful of exceptions, they all chose winter. I was flabbergasted! While parents were grumbling about colds, flu, icy roads, and gloomy skies, these kids came up with all kinds of reasons why winter is wonderful (Christmas! Hanukkah! Snow angels! Skating!). It dawned on me that this since this project was done in midwinter, the children would naturally gravitate toward the present season as their favorite, since kids are so "in the moment." If the bar graph project had been done in any other season, that would likely be the one chosen as the hands-down favorite.

As we grow into adulthood, many of us lose touch with a natural connection to the seasons and the unique pleasures of each. Our culture gives us few reasons—or reminders—to live according to seasonal rhythms. It's odd that the most intense period of celebrating and socializing occurs right around the winter solstice, when darkness falls at an unreasonably early hour. High spirits, frantic shopping, nonstop preparation, last-minute travel, and perpetual hubbub rule the human world just as all of nature and its creatures begin a period of dormancy. That post-holiday letdown many people experience may not be so much due to the holidays ending, but rather to fighting the natural inclination toward quiet and retreat during the darkest days of the year.

Conversely, many of us spend entire summers in climate-con-trolled offices when we should be lounging in hammocks, going on picnics, swimming, and socializing. I'm not sure what can be done about this—there's no movement, as far as I know, to move winter holidays to July, nor one that would allow those with full-time jobs to take entire summers off. In parts of the world down under, like Australia and New Zealand, Christmas is celebrated at the height of summer; in Europe, the long summer holiday is a fact of life.

Obstacles aside, it's entirely possible to reacquaint ourselves with the natural cycles of the year and celebrate the unique qualities of each season as it comes around. For those of us who are not too religious, celebrating the start of each season can offer an alternative to denominational rites. Natural cycles impact on our physical, emotional, and psychological well-being. By just being more aware of the seasons, we regain our sense of wonder for them. Reinforcing your children's intuitive interest in seasonal changes is great motivation for heightening your own awareness.

Nature activities through the seasons

Observing the natural world keeps our sense of awe alive. Wonder comes in all sizes, from a graceful hummingbird or a spider spinning its web, to a solar eclipse or a desert canyon. If you haven't got the time or inclination for mountain biking or white-water rafting, and if the whole notion of "adventure vacations" is an oxymoron as far as you're concerned, fear not. The natural world can be enjoyed in a variety of small, tame doses.

   Some children take to nature—well, naturally. Others balk and complain ("It's too buggy!" "I'm bored!" "My legs are tired!"). For the latter, especially, constructing enjoyable traditions around nature outings can be key to ensuring mutual enjoyment. A favorite, familiar place at which the children can enjoy predictable yet pleasurable activities helps ensure anticipation rather than angst. If you'd like your children to gain a greater appreciation for nature, try designing rituals around the following and other outdoor activities you already enjoy. Tie them into a special place or particular season; pack a picnic to help turn these outings into traditions:

✧ Most kids love to be on the water. Rent a boat, canoe, or kayak, and find out in advance what you can expect to observe, for example, a rookery (bird-hatching area). Teach your kids to take great care while visiting these ecologically sensitive areas.

✧ To add enticement to outdoor adventures, especially for younger children, play games such as scavenger hunt or "I spy." Bring items to sharpen the power of observation— sketchbooks (for quick sketches and leaf rubbings), disposable cameras, binoculars, and magnifying glasses. Guides to identify wildflowers, leaves, or wild mushrooms are enticing to older children.

✧ Go on an organized bird-watching expedition. See what child-friendly events your local Audubon Society sponsors each year. Or, participate in a hawk or eagle watch. Bird-related activities are year-round events. Log onto the Audubon Society to find a local chapter near you.

✧ Explore the teeming life of a pond or swamp in early spring; look for turtles, frogs, waterfowl and their young. Bring small nets and containers (fill them with water from the pond) to scoop out and observe animal life, but put everything right back afterwards.

✧ In midsummer, take a trip to a butterfly garden or conservatory. Make sure to give each child a guide to help them see how many varieties they can find.

✧ Visit a botanical garden or arboretum. Late spring is an especially good time, with flowering trees in bloom. Give children a map and assign each one to find specific plants or trees. Make this into a noncompetitive game, but do offer a reward of an ice cream or some other enticing small perk.

✧ Spring, summer, or fall are all good seasons for hiking to a waterfall or a modest summit, then taking in the view while enjoying a picnic. Make sure to bring some of the aforementioned tools—magnifiying glasses, binoculars, and such, to make the journey more interesting for the young.

✧ Be backyard astronomers—make regular dates to observe the night sky. Subscribe to "Sky Tips," an e-newsletter provided by Star Date Online (www. StarDate.org); find out what to look for in the sky each month.

✧ In different locales, and at various times of the year, take your kids on a hunt for "nature's art supplies." Collect leaves, curly vines, seeds, and pinecones in autumn woods; search for smooth pebbles along rivers or streams; pick up seashells, driftwood, and sea glass along a shoreline. Use care and common sense to determine what can be collected and taken home. Once home, do art projects with your finds: leaf rubbings, pinecone swags, seed pictures, seashell necklaces, sea glass mosaics.

Spring planting traditions

Those of us in four-season climates have seen spring return dozens of times, yet it's impossible not to feel awed each time it arrives. Spring exemplifies hope, renewal, and possibility. As we emerge from winter's hibernation, our minds burst with new projects, plans, and ambitions. An urge to clear, clean, and start anew takes over, making room to sow seeds, both literally and figuratively. These "seeds" are symbolic of creative ideas and desires that have yet to unfold and that, with luck, will flourish in the seasons ahead. Spring is the season to emerge, explore, feed the senses, and feel wonder. Planting activities are metaphoric for the sense of renewal that each spring brings:

✧ On the first day of spring, have a seed-planting ceremony. Start seedlings indoors for container gardens or planting outdoors later in the season. Tomatoes, herbs, vegetables, and flowers all hold the possibility of summer pleasures. Miniature "greenhouse kits," available at garden centers, make the process easy and exciting. Or go the old-fashioned route with egg crates, potting soil, and judicious watering.

✧ Follow up by finding out the exact date in your region when it's safe to transfer young plants outdoors. Hold an annual planting day for the new plants sown from seed.

✧ Each year, create at least one festive garden project with a child, such as a container vegetable garden, a miniature desertscape, or a flowering window box. A splendid source for these and other easy garden projects is *My First Garden Book* (Dorling Kindersley, 1992).

✧ Take an annual outing to a park, arboretum, or botanical garden and let your eyes feast on flowering trees like cherry, dogwood, and magnolia. If you have access to these kinds of trees, such as on your own or a friend's property, carefully prune a few branches to bring indoors, and display them in a vase.

✧ Repot indoor plants that have become pot bound. Potted plants are often constrained after winter, and need more room to grow—just as we do after a winter spent mainly indoors.

✧ Create a festive centerpiece of budding branches of pussy willows, freesia, or forsythia. Surround these with one or more vases of daisies, lilies, and irises. Delicate, budlike flowers are always welcome, as are pots of flowering bulbs.

Planting wishes

When my daughters were young, we had an annual tradition of planting what we called a "wish garden." It was actually a sneaky way for me to start seedlings of plants I wanted to transfer into the garden, like tomatoes, peppers, carrots, parsley, and annual flowers.

Each of the girls would get to plant a seed in one of the compartments of a foam egg carton. We would label them not only to identify what kind of plants they'd become, but each plant corresponded with a "wish" from numbers one through twelve. We'd write the wishes down on a piece of paper. The only rule was that the wishes couldn't be material things. I didn't want this to become another Christmas list. They were more like "I wish my front tooth would grow back by June," or "I wish I could visit Natasha" (a friend who had moved away).

After the seeds germinated, and before we transferred them into bigger pots to plant outside, we'd see which three of their twelve plants were the biggest. Those were the wishes that would come true. And oddly enough, most of those wishes did come true!

—Sarah Margolin

Springtime is perfect for picnics

A delicious meal eaten outdoors—deliberately planned, at any time of year—is a perfect springboard for creating tradition. One of my favorite warm-season rituals is seeking out wonderful new places to combine an outdoor adventure with a picnic. Fortunately, I live in a region that offers a life's supply of remarkable picnic spots. When my husband and I first moved here from New York City, we didn't even wait for spring before embarking on our first picnic. Taking advantage of an unseasonably warm January day, we enjoyed an outdoor meal at an exquisite land preserve—a spot to which we've returned many times, in every season, to hike and picnic. Each year, on the first truly warm and beautiful weekend day (whether that day happens to fall in April or in June), we make a ritual of packing a picnic and taking it to one of several favorite spots.

It may have been sneaky, but when our sons were young, we always found that they were more enticed by nature outings if we called them "picnics" rather than "hikes." Now that our sons are older, and immune to such subterfuge, the pleasure of returning to a well-loved place and following a familiar routine with well-stocked knapsacks has not lost its charm.

My friend Sue shared an offbeat story of a family picnic tradition. From the time she was about seven years old, her parents and siblings had weekly "opposite season" picnics at a public lake about an hour from their Michigan home, no matter what the weather. Most vivid in her memory are images of the family tromping through snow, wind, and rain, doing a "wood hunt" for dried twigs with which to start a fire in the barbecue pit. After a fire-roasted lunch, they did some sort of physical activity—a long walk, if weather permitted; skating or sledding in the winter. The weekly picnic continued until Sue was in her mid-thirties, with two children of her own, allowing regular, anticipated time for her parents to connect with their grandkids. Once her parents moved to California, the ritual ended, since they'd been the driving force behind it. The cold-weather picnics are among Sue's fondest childhood memories, and she hopes her own children, now grown as well, share the feeling.

Some picnic adventures are invigorating, others are relaxing and meditative. One of our favorite places is a Buddhist monastery with pagoda-like structures set among simple gardens and ponds. The monastery welcomes picnickers, but cautions that "vegetarian rules apply." Buddhist monasteries and other contemplative retreats can be found in the most surprising of areas; see if there's one near you, and inquire in advance if they welcome day visitors.

✧ State and national landmarks are also fun, combining a good outdoor meal with a gentle lesson in history. Nearby, the Hudson River is lined with the mansions and gardens of nineteenth-century industrialists and political figures like the Vanderbilts and Roosevelts. Now open to the public, these venues welcome visitors and their picnic supplies. Do a little research on historic sites in your area. Many welcome visitors bearing food by offering designated picnic areas; often, these sites also have lovely gardens or trails to explore as well.

✧ A hike at a nature preserve is sure to whet the appetite. For some, nothing appeals more than a picnic at a beach. For more sophisticated tastes or when picnicking with a special sweetheart, have your outdoor meal with an open air concert. River banks, waterfalls, arboretums, and even beautifully landscaped college campuses offer sensory pleasures lasting long after the last morsel is consumed.

✧ For families with young children, an ideal spot for a casual picnic with little ones is a community park, combined with a visit to a great playground. Similarly, combining a lake shore picnic with swimming, boating, or kite flying makes the experience more appealing to younger kids.

✧ While spring may be the perfect time for a picnic ritual, heralding as it does the arrival of warm season pleasures, autumn is also a splendid time for combining picnics with hikes, and not just for the obvious enjoyment of the splendid colors. The slight chill in the air is perfectly suited to a hiker's gear and garb. And the shifting quality of autumn's light—suddenly more shadowy than summer's warm glow—is an urgent reminder to savor what's left before those shorter days set in.

As for the food . . .

✧ For some, a picnic is mainly about the food, but not for me. I can recall every exquisite place where I've enjoyed an outdoor meal, but I'd be hard pressed to tell you what I ate. A picnic can be just as blissful with sandwiches and juice as with fancier fare and wine. I like to think of the food as parallel to the experience itself: Simple, healthy, and unpretentious.

✧ The meal should be easy to serve and taste good at room temperature. Light dishes that provide quick energy to sustain a walk, hike, or swim are the cornerstones of a wholesome picnic menu. A too-heavy meal might put you more in the mood for a nap than for activity!

✧ Over the years, I've developed a formula of sorts for the meal, so it's easy for me to pack a picnic, even on the spur of a moment: Start with a good bread and a tasty spread (packed separately in a container); add two hearty salads (potato salad is always welcome, as are grain salads). Finish with fresh fruit (washed ahead of time and packed into containers), an optional dessert (nothing gooey!), and plenty of beverages.

✧ If your picnic plans are too last-minute to make even a simple meal, consider buying an assortment of good-quality pre-pared salads, spreads, and relishes at a deli counter or specialty grocery. Treat yourself to a meal with a theme, such as Middle Eastern: store-bought hummus, fresh pita bread, cured olives, stuffed grape leaves, and tabouleh salad are perfect for a fuss-free outdoor meal.

As the years pass, my penchant for picnics remains unabated. It's just as fine a form of relaxation and renewal with a family in tow as it was when it was just the two of us. As our sons have grown, our family has enjoyed picnics at beaches, waterfalls, national historic landmarks, and botanic gardens. A lovely vista, some not-too-rigorous physical activity, and simple, tasty fare are the prime ingredients for a perfect picnic. Making them a regular part of seasonal forays, and returning to favorite places helps elevate picnics to ritual status. The experience is trans-formed from merely eating lunch outdoors to a refreshing lift for the spirit and senses.

We had a marvelous picnic, high up over the Connecticut Valley in a field. We spread our blanket in the shade at the edge of the woods, and spent a heavenly hour, absorbing the hazy gentle hills, the open space, the presence of the river with its nineteenth-century atmosphere.

—May Sarton,
Journal of a Solitude

Summer relaxation rituals

In many Asian traditions, summer's symbolic element, not surprisingly, is fire. The gradual awakening of spring segues (sometimes too quickly) into a period of heat and radiance. Summer's fiery energy is expansive—it invites you to play, enjoy friends, travel. The world around us is zesty, delicious, and abundant. Blossoming gives way to ripening. As the fruits of the earth ripen, so can the dreams and projects that started as seeds in the spring. See if you can nurture what you've sown, both literally and figuratively.

✧ Have an annual family camp-out, even if it's in your own back yard. Have a campfire, and set up tents. Enjoy a cookout, then stay up late telling stories and stargazing.

✧ Set up pots of fresh herbs in a sunny windowsill, or on a porch or deck. If you prefer not to grow your own, make sure to buy fragrant bunches at farm markets to embellish summer fare.

✧ Make a tradition of deliberately choosing to learn something new each summer. I like to brush up on foreign languages; maybe you'd like to brush up on your favorite periods in history, read political or literary biographies, or tackle a new craft or skill.

✧ Make a yearly ceremony of changing your home decor: Cover your sofas with cotton slipcovers, and your beds with cool cotton sheets and blankets. Place lots of bright flowers in every available vase, in every room of the house.

✧ Summer food traditions include fresh corn on the cob, berries, melons, and other luscious fruits, tomatoes, and more tomatoes! Feed your palate's preference for minimally cooked, light foods with cold soups, veggie-filled wraps, and bountiful salads. Wash it all down with homemade lemonade, and top it off with ice cream.

✧ During any beach visits, collect sea glass, shells, pebbles, and driftwood. Do art projects with your children from your finds—sea glass mosaics, shell-covered picture frames, or drift-wood mobiles.

✧ At the end of summer, make a simple memory book of the summer's activities and adventures. During the course of the summer, save memorabilia in a box—camp and vacation pictures, ticket stubs, travel brochures, postcards, and other paraphernalia. Use a quiet, rainy morning to glue them into an attractive blank journal.

Beach traditions, local outings, and vacations at home: Some of the most evocative childhood memories are made of sand and sun. Somehow, time spent at the beach becomes a cherished tradition for those lucky enough to have access to a shoreline. Carolyn has been going to Cape Cod nearly every summer since she was a child, and has been taking her daughter, Chelsea, there for at least one week each summer to enjoy the same things she did when she was young. They bike into town or take the path to Provincetown, go on a whale watch and to the Audubon Society, and walk on their favorite rocky beach. The warm bays and ponds, the beauty of the light and colors, and the air's briny scent add up to a cherished tradition that Carolyn can't imagine doing without, even but for one week each summer. At the age of fourteen, Chelsea already appreciates the lure of the familiar, and can envision continuing the ritual into her own adulthood.

Beth's family enjoys an enviable week-long mini-reunion at the end of each summer—six side-by-side cottages on the Jersey Shore for her family, and the families of her two sisters, her husband's brother, and each set of their parents. The days consist of cousins playing together, parents relaxing together, cooperatively made barbecue dinners, and lots of reading.

Traditional summer outings: Having at least one must-do summer outing—something old-fashioned, bordering on corny—can make the season complete. You probably already have a favorite summer activity or two. Elevate them to the status of tradition and see how much more satisfying they can be. Consider your family's preferences and interests; try a few of these outings on for size. Decide whether your special outing traditions will be solely for your own family, or a chance to join forces with another family. Here are a few possibilities:

✧ Attend one major league baseball game.

✧ Pile into the car for a drive-in movie.

✧ Attend an old-fashioned country fair.

✧ Ferry to an island for a picnic.

✧ Take a long, leisurely bicycle ride on a favorite trail.

✧ Attend an outdoor theater performance, concert, or Shakespeare festival.

Be a tourist in your own town: Adventure trips are good, taking you out of your comfort zone, though admittedly, they are work (the word *travel* is derived from the French *travaille,* which in fact, means work). Families with young children, lots of children, or those who simply can't get away in the summer might enjoy a tradition of being "tourists" at home. Designate a day each week, or a long weekend, to visit places you never seem to get to when you're in work-and-school mode, such as museums, historic sites, and recreational areas. Eat dinner at new or favorite restaurants, get tickets to summer stock theater or an outdoor concert. Pack a picnic for lunch and explore an out-of-the-way waterfall; take a tour by bicycle; hop on a train or ferry to poke around a neighboring town that you never seem to get around to visiting.

Rituals for Our Times authors Evan Imber-Black and Janine Roberts describe a family that plans a "vacation at home" each year. This family of six found that they came back from their vacations exhausted and feeling that they had spent too much money. Instead, they began spending a yearly vacation at home. They prepared favorite foods ahead of time, ate out more than usual, and made a commitment to put off chores, turn off the phone, and limit TV. Each day they did a nearby activity that they all looked forward to. Getting into vacation mode while at home does take a certain amount of discipline, but is an effort worth making when going further afield is not an option. Packing the day with local activities that you rarely get around to, and ending up in your own beds, can be perfectly blissful.

fall festivities

In Chinese tradition, the earth's energy is said to begin pulling inward and contracting. Fall brings conflicting emotions: On one hand, it's somewhat dispiriting when darkness falls at 5:00 by the end of October, with only shorter, colder days to look forward to for some time. On the other hand, nippy air can be so welcome following summer's heat. Parents feel mixed emotions as their children return to school—we miss their presence and the open days of summer, yet it's nice to have more time for ourselves. Fall's themes of harvest or gathering can be applied to our personal endeavors. Like gathering the season's abundant crops, we can also reap what has blossomed in our lives throughout the year.

✧ If you're lucky enough to have a fireplace in your home, make the first one of the season a special occasion. Make a hearty seasonal stew, or pumpkin bread and cider to enjoy before a roaring fire. Cait Johnson, in *Celebrating the Great Mother,* writes that she throws a handful of sea salt and a couple of bay leaves into the season's first fire as symbols of protection.

✧ An early fall "moon viewing party" has long been a tradition in Japan. Each September, shrines and other community organizations celebrate Kangetsu-sai to celebrate the beauty of the harvest moon with traditional music, dancing, poetry, and blessings. Have your own "moon viewing" ritual by taking autumn walks in the light of the full moon.

✧ Celebrate leaves! Go on an annual "leaf-peeping" expedition, following a familiar route to observe the changing landscape.

Collect colorful leaves and press them in heavy books between sheets of waxed paper. Have your kids make leaf rubbings. Make a leaf pile for your children to jump into; jump into it yourself!

✧ Each fall, make a date with your family to plant lots of bulbs for perennials that will emerge the following spring. Show children pictures of what they can expect to pop out of the ground after the snow melts.

✧ Decorate your home with farmstand finds: Use pumpkins, squashes, Indian corn, gourds, and fall flowers like mums and asters to make arrangements in your kitchen, on your porch, and indeed any place in your home that would benefit from these predict-able, yet perennially pleasing arrangements.

✧ Prepare jars of grains, dried beans, whole-grain flours, dried fruits, nuts, and seeds. Just as the animal world performs its annual rite of putting away stores of food for the coming colder months, you too can enjoy a wholesome annual ritual of gathering and storing. For this, I use quart-sized mason jars, available by the case in any hardware or agricultural supply store. I also display them prominently on my kitchen shelves, as a reminder to use these nourish-ing foods as often as possible.

✧ Late fall is pumpkin season. Take your kids to a pumpkin patch and select sugar pumpkins for baking pies, making soups and stews, and incorporating into sweet quick breads and muffins. Choose large pumpkins for jack-o-lanterns or for simply setting at your doorstep. Enjoy hot apple cider with fresh pumpkin bread. Attend an autumn harvest or pumpkin festival. They often pair seasonal food and wonderful music, backdropped by dazzling foliage.

Pumpkin festival

Each year, my family and I go to Keene, New Hampshire, the weekend before Halloween to attend their annual Pumpkin Festival. This festival holds the world's record for having the most pumpkins lit at one time. It's quite elaborate, with two twelve-story scaffoldings filled with lit pumpkins of all sizes and carved with varying degrees of skill. The festival starts off with a parade and is filled with food, activities for kids, pony rides, and firecrackers.

During the parade, all the kids in costume march around the town, leading to downtown; all of the merchants stand outside their doors passing out treats. My husband's mother makes my son's and daughter's costumes. Now that Pedro is old enough, he can help decide on what kind of costume he wants. Pedro participates in the parade holding his dad's hand while I take pictures. Last year, he was the only Batman, and baby Amelia was a flowered bunny with floppy ears and a bushy tail.

When we return home, I unpack the costumes and put them away for safekeeping. It will be for them to decide what to do with them when they get older—maybe give them to their own kids for Halloween costumes or for dress-up. I thought it would be a neat thing to save for them; if nothing else, the costumes will bring back wonderful memories of our annual trip to Keene's Pumpkin Festival.

—Sylvia Diaz

Warming winter traditions

Winter's themes are dormancy and regeneration. By honoring rather than fighting this quieter part of the natural cycle, you'll be ever more ready for the blossoming of spring. Unless you're the type who begins waxing her skis as soon as the first snowflake falls, the ideal antidote to winter's chill and gloom is to turn inward and give in to the natural tendency to retreat.

Instead of feeling frustrated by the cold, dark period from January to March, try to savor a slower pace, and incorporate more deliberate solitude and quiet time into your days. Teach your children to do the same. It can be a delightful time to retreat to the shelter of home and hearth and get things done without the distractions afforded by the other seasons. Direct your focus inward to stay in balance, and break the season's monotony with fun, comforting treats.

✧ If a snowstorm is headed your way, prepare for a relaxing snow day with a 1000- or 1500-piece jigsaw puzzle, some good-quality cocoa for making hot chocolate, a few entertaining videos and good books, and plenty of wood, if you have a fireplace or wood stove.

✧ Stop fighting the snow and have some fun with it—go sledding, snow shoeing, or cross-country skiing; take a walk in the silence of winter woods. Do corny snow activities with your partner or kids—make snowmen, snow angels, snow ice cream. Lisa Ross and her kids take spray bottles with food coloring in water and "write" on the snow.

✧ Put up nesting boxes and bird feeders for wintering birds. You'll be astonished at the number of birds that remain in cold areas for the winter, and at the amount of pleasure gained from observing them. You'll find everything you need to know about feeding and sheltering wintering birds at the Cornell Lab of Ornithology, http://www.birds.cornell.edu/programs/AllAboutBirds/AttractingBirds/FeedingBirds/FeedPestsPredators.html

✧ Indulge in regular rituals of self-care. Take lots of baths, pamper your skin with soothing creams and oils, and comfort your winter-parched feet with special soaks.

✧ Have staples on hand to cook comforting soups and stews all season. To create a soup tradition, have a weekly "soup and bread night" all winter. Make sure you have your favorite seasonings on hand—an all-purpose seasoning mix, good-quality curry powder, an Italian seasoning blend are among those I find indispensable. Add good pot and ladle, attractive soup bowls or crocks, and some great recipes and you're set for the season.

✧ Many of us approach winter solstice—the shortest day of the year— with dread. On the flip side, though, the day marks the beginning of light returning as the sun starts moving northward again. Winter solstice is part of the ancient tradition of Yule, celebrated December 20 to 23. Many people like to use this time to decorate their Christmas tree and put up lots of lights. Others fill their homes with lit candles, build a bonfire, or sing and tell stories about the sun.

Yule pleasures

For the winter solstice, or Yule, which usually falls just before Christmas (which we also celebrate), we light all the candles we can find in the house and set up bowls with apples and nuts for our guests. We also make "Bubble Wish Bread." We roll bread dough into little balls, and as we roll we think and talk about our wishes and dreams for the coming year. The balls are layered into a bundt pan with a sweet glaze and nuts. The resulting bread is a sweet, messy delight, and fun to eat by candlelight! In addition to hopes for the future, we focus on gratitude for things in our life by making a paper apple chain out of green and red construction paper. On each apple we take turns writing something we are thankful for or some good memory from the past year. We hang this above a double doorway where we can look up and remember throughout the season.

—Melanie Wilson

Winter "cabin fever" fun

If you have preschoolers or young school-age children home on snow days and sick days, creating special "cabin fever" rituals will help you actually look forward to, rather than dread, those long days at home. Some mothers keep a "cabin fever" drawer filled with special games, toys, and treats that come out only on these occasions, lending an otherwise gloomy day a festive air. When my children were young, snow days would mean pulling out a favorite "kitchen chemistry" book. The boys would be excited and occupied experimenting with baking soda and vinegar, cornstarch and water, food coloring and milk. Once that mess was cleaned up, we'd start a new one with some cooking or baking activities. Several cold, home-bound days in a row can be challenging for parents of young children, but activities specifically designated for these kinds of days can make them feel more like a cozy retreat. Here are some simple ideas:

✧ On the most dismal February day possible, plan a festive indoor picnic. Take a break from the predictable comfort foods of the season and have the kids help prepare an array of light finger foods, sandwiches, potato salad, and lemonade. Spread a blanket and, if possible, have the picnic before a cheering fire.

✧ Similarly, plan an annual indoor camping trip just when everyone has really had it with winter, or be ready to have one when a snowstorm is predicted. Borrow a few beautifully photographed books on national parks or other natural wonders from the library. Decide where you are "going" for your trip by browsing through the books (and in the process, learning about some amazing places). Bring out the sleeping bags and air mattresses; pitch a small pup tent if you have one. Plan a cookout-style meal and tell great stories around a "campfire" (a real roaring fire in your fireplace, or an imagined campfire). Use no incandescent lights (candles or flashlights are fine). Have everyone sleep in the living room or family room. This winter spirit-lifter can be great fun even for those who don't care for real camping trips!

✧ Prepare a box of letter-writing supplies especially for these kinds of stay-at-home days. Have the kids make beautiful cards using collage materials, stamp kits, stickers, and scented markers. Craft stores are a good source for blank cards and the aforementioned supplies. Once the cards are made, have the children write letters and notes to distant relatives and friends. Make a ceremony out of taking all the mail to the post office. The fun is extended if the kids start getting replies! For more ideas on letter writing rituals, see The Lost Art of Letter Writing, page 128.

✧ Just before the winter holidays begin, visit a local thrift shop and stock up on dress-up clothes. Around the time of the holidays, these shops tend to have fancier and more offbeat items that are perfect for this sort of endeavor. Make sure to include accessories like scarves, belts, and hats. After the clothes are cleaned, find a special container for them, like a wicker laundry basket or a toy chest. Take it out on a day when the winter blues descend, and watch the fun begin. Let the kids do what kids do best and just pretend, or encourage them to make up skits.

✧ When my sons were young and cabin fever hit hard, I always turned to the one indoor activity that never seemed to lose its charm—baking projects. Homemade cookies, muffins, and quick breads go a long way toward brightening days when you feel that winter will never end. If you are a bit more ambitious, cabin fever days are the perfect occasions to try the long, slow process of making yeasted breads with your kids (see Playing in the dough, page 26). Enjoying warm, wholesome treats fresh from the oven nourishes body, soul, and senses at once.

Resources

Celebrating the Great Mother: A Handbook of Earth-Honoring Activities for Parents and Children by Cait Johnson and Maura Shaw (Destiny Books, 1995). This book is a fantastic resource for earth-centered seasonal celebrations. These include solstices, equinoxes, Yule, Ostara, Beltane, and others, with crafts, activities, blessings, meditations, and more, all geared to families with young and older children.

Cracked Corn and Snow Ice Cream: A Family Almanac by Nancy Willard (Harcourt, Brace and Co., 1997). This beautifully designed and illustrated country almanac takes the reader through the year with significant dates, bucolic lore, projects, and recipes.

Nature's Art Box: From T-Shirts to Twig Baskets, 65 Cool Projects for Crafty Kids to Make with Natural Materials You Can Find Anywhere by Laura C. Martin (Storey Publishing, 2003). If you're trying to tempt your kids to venture into the natural world, this book provides ample incentive.

Nature in a Nutshell for Kids: Over 100 Activities You Can Do in Ten Minutes or Less by Jean Potter (John Wiley and Sons, 1995). Same comment as the one above—another fun resource.

Cooking Art: Easy Edible Art for Young Children by Mary Ann F. Kohl and Jean Potter (Gryphon House, 1997) is an adorable book filled with simple and rewarding cooking projects to do with little ones, great for "cabin fever" diversions.

Seasonal food pleasures

A growing movement in my region encourages people to use at least one locally grown food each day. At a time when small farmers are struggling to survive, this helps local economies and is a more sustainable practice than continually buying food trucked into supermarkets over thousands of miles.

The call to use one local food per day has gotten me to thinking about how drastically my own shopping habits have changed over the last few years. I pick up my family's share of just-picked organic produce once a week from May through November at the CSA (Community Supported Agriculture) farm we belong to; I shop at a local natural foods store once or twice a week for fruits and veggies I can't get at the CSA, as well as other staples for my (rapidly) growing sons; and in season, I visit local farm markets on a regular basis.

My new food-gathering habits have become pleasant rituals. I enjoy chatting with the growers and fellow members at the CSA. Supporting local businesses like Mother Earth's, the natural foods market, feels better than traipsing the aisles of impersonal supermarkets. I always chat with the employees, and often sip a cup of organic coffee or freshly made juice while I shop. I don't really need to shop at farm markets, but that, too, is a pleasant ritual, and helps support the efforts of small, family-owned businesses.

Using seasonal (and ideally, organic and local) produce and ingredients, you can create meals that dazzle the eyes and palate and are incredibly simple to prepare. Eating with the seasons not only helps foster rewarding food traditions, but benefits the environment. Supporting sustainable agriculture reduces our dependence on imported produce, and in effect, the energy required to transport it and the pesticides used to grow it.

It may not be practical to eliminate supermarket shopping (after all, we do need our tissues, paper towels, and such), but think of ways in which you can "localize" at least some of your food shopping, especially during warmer months. Take full advantage of local foods by joining a CSA farm, shopping at farmer's markets, and picking your own produce. All are superb experiences to share with children, allowing them to see the connection between their foods and their source.

Community Supported Agriculture: What exactly is Community Supported Agriculture? The University of Massachusetts Extension defines it as "a partnership of mutual commitment between a farm and a community of supporters which provides a direct link between the production and consumption of food. Supporters cover a farm's yearly operating budget by purchasing a share of the season's harvest. CSA members make a commitment to support the farm throughout the season, and assume the costs, risks, and bounty of growing food along with the farmer or grower." The numbers of community farms has grown tremendously just over the last decade; there are hundreds in the U.S. alone.

Apart from the obvious benefit of freshly harvested organic produce and special events, it seems to me that CSA members most enjoy the ritual of the share pickup, chatting with the growers and fellow members, seeing what produce is new that week, enjoying the scents and colors, then taking it home to the kitchen. CSAs also foster a sense of community. The one I belong to holds regular potlucks on the farm to connect members, honor the growers and interns, and share food made from the produce. The farm also serves as a springboard for various outreach and charitable activities, and is a catalyst for further social bonds.

To make a peach you need a winter, a summer, an autumn, and a bee, so many nights and days and sun and rain, petals rosy with pollen—all that your mouth may know a few minutes of pleasure.

—Anonymous

Ask around out about CSAs in your area that you might join. They're available in urban areas, not just in the countryside. To find a CSA in your area, search the database at Alternative Farming Systems Information Center, www.nal.usda.gov/afsic/csa.

Preserving summer

A lot of people probably think I'm crazy—you can buy a jar of good pasta sauce at the grocery store for a few dollars, so why go to all the trouble of making and canning my own? This is the way I mark the passing of summer to autumn; it reconnects me with my days of growing up on a farm, when we had to preserve the fall harvest for the coming winter months.

The money I may (or may not) save is the least of it. Far more important is the trip to our local farmer's market where I have discovered the sweetest old man who grows the sweetest tomatoes ever. I love to just look at all the perfectly laid out tomatoes at his stand. After buying boxes of tomatoes, I scour around for a fragrant stand with basil, another with garlic, and finally, one with sweet onions.

Then, it's off to my kitchen where I begin chopping, dicing, and cooking the tomatoes down to a thick, rich paste. Outside my kitchen window, I note how the sunlight has taken a decided shift to the south; no longer does it come in my north-facing windows like it does all summer. Once the tomatoes are simmering, I begin sautéing the garlic and onions in olive oil. Then, I add the tomatoes and fresh herbs and allow the whole mess to stew a little longer before sealing it in mason jars. Once the sauce is canned, it's perfectly safe to take the jars down to the basement for storage, but I always let them linger on the kitchen counter for a few days—probably to show off just a bit, yet also to admire as my personal signal of summer's passing.

—Mary Rogers

Farmer's markets: Hothouse tomatoes, waxed apples, rock-hard peaches, shower-soaked lettuces—welcome to the supermarket produce section. Though this venue for fresh food has improved over the last few years, primped, prepackaged fruits and veggies still serve as reminders that mass-produced produce is bred to look good and last long, rather than taste good. Meant to withstand long rides on trucks and planes, hard and sturdy, not lush and ripe, are the watchwords.

While most supermarket produce sections are serviceable (where would we be without them in winter?), they can't compare with the colorful, fragrant offerings from farm markets and roadside produce stands. Just-picked produce bursts with fragrance and invites touching and comparing. Here's one instance where impulse buying and letting your senses rule is half the fun. After all, turban squash, fiddlehead ferns, or a peck of habañero peppers may never appear on your shopping list. Farmer's markets have proliferated in rural as well as urban areas every-

where, so chances are there's one near you. You'll not only enjoy produce that's fresher and riper that anything mass produced, but you will cast a vote for small farms and sustainable agriculture with each dollar you spend.

Farm market excursions are wonderful outings to take with children, who enjoy meeting and talking to the people who produce their food. Visiting a local farmer's market (or taking a field trip to go from one farm stand to another) once a week can easily become a favorite summer and fall tradition. Once you find your favorite stands and get to know the farmers, you'll surely grow to regard these weekly excursions as a favorite food-gathering ritual.

✧ Deborah recalls a memorable apple-picking outing taken with her family and two others. On a hilltop overlooking the orchard, they segued into a spontaneous picnic, and literally enjoyed the fruits of their labor. Juicy, just-picked apples were washed at outdoor taps and accompanied by sharp cheddar cheese, pumpkin bread, and cider, purchased from the orchard's market. It was a delicious afternoon, in every sense. Having made apple and pear picking a yearly ritual, Deborah stores the fruit in a large wicker basket on her kitchen floor. Most are eaten out of hand, some made into applesauce, apple or pear cake, and miniature tarts.

✧ Wendy and her husband began an annual apple-picking ritual when their first son was a Snugli-wrapped infant. Twelve years and three additional children later, a year has not gone by with at least one, and usually more, fruit-picking outings. The family most often frequented a nearby apple farm, spending an entire day, complete with picnic and gorgeous views of a river valley. Now that the family is concerned with the pesticide issue, they prefer to visit farms where they can pick organic berries. What is most appealing, she says, is reaping and gathering food directly from its source—a process we don't get to experience at the supermarket. Wendy has often extended the pleasure of berry-picking outings by making and canning jam—one big batch per fruit picking, ensuring her family the enjoyment of delicious jam all winter.

Resources

Local Flavors: Cooking and Eating from America's Farm Markets by Deborah Madison (Broadway Books, 2002) features not only recipes but lots of personal musings about the noted chef's visits to 100 farmer's markets.

The Greenmarket Cookbook: Recipes, Tips, and Lore from the World Famous Urban Farmers' Market by Joel Patraker, Joan Schwartz (Viking Press, 2000) gathers recipes and tips from one of the oldest and largest American farm markets.

Preserving Summer's Bounty: A Quick and Easy Guide to Freezing, Canning, Preserving, and Drying What You Grow by Susan McClure (Rodale Books, 1998) is a good guide for those who wish to extend the summer food-gathering season.

Part five
friendship rituals

A friend is one to whom one may pour out all the contents of one's heart, chaff and grain together, knowing that gentle hands will take and sift it, keep what is worth keeping, and with a breath of kindness, blow the rest away.

—George Eliot

Standing dates with friends

When I ask friends how they are, they're more likely to describe how busy they are than to tell me how they're feeling. Whether they have kids or not, work at home or outside it, all have calendars straining at the margins. Whenever I feel overly busy, I need only to compare my schedule with that of my friends, whose tales of orchestrating their own jam-packed schedules as well as their children's far outpace mine. Single women, similarly, are no slouches at filling up every waking hour. While catching up with a cousin not long ago, my head spun from her tales of juggling a full-time nursing job with live music gigs and magazine-writing assignments.

Remember the days when you could just call up a friend and say, "Let's meet in town for coffee in fifteen minutes"? Few women I know can exercise such spontaneity. Instead, we pore over our appointment books, searching for that elusive hour, two weeks hence, when we might squeeze in a short visit. Seeing your closest friends only when you can squeeze one another into your packed schedule offers neither routine nor ritual.

Especially during the hectic years of child rearing, it becomes increasingly difficult to find time for easy, regular time with friends. And that's when we need our friends most! Setting up standing dates, whether with one dear friend or a group, helps assure that those treasured friendships don't get lost in the day to day.

Standing dates are regularly scheduled times to meet somewhere specific, do something special, or accomplish some shared purpose. Firmly scheduled gatherings take the planning and stress out of maintaining friendships. Two, three, or more friends can plan to meet once a week, or once a month. If it's the same time, same place, and a specific activity, little or no advance planning is needed. For many women, "girlfriend rituals" offer a much-needed break from family time, while others might include the kids if that's more practical. Recently, I passed by a tiny café during lunchtime and noticed at least a dozen strollers parked outside. I later found out that once a week, the owner gives over the entire place to mothers and their babies and toddlers!

Though the hunger is strong for good friends to convene on a regular basis, the opportunities to do so regularly and easily (like the kitchen-table confabulations and coffee-klatches of previous generations) are increasingly rare. Just being with friends is somehow not enough for busy women. We also want the rare time spent away from our own families to be constructive —discussing literature, knitting sweaters, or working out.

Still, it's perfectly fine to have a regular "girl's night out" for its own sake. Mary has been going out to dinner with a group of friends for twelve years. "We went out to dinner once a month when our kids were little because we were so desperate to put on some decent clothes and get out for an evening," she says. "Now, we only get together every two or three months for lunch, but it is still every bit as enjoyable. There's nothing like longtime friends."

Pressed for time, friends often look for something of value to share—a bit of culture gleaned from a book group, serenity from a meditation group, or fresh air and exercise from regular walks. Even if it's just going out—or staying in—with a group of good friends, as in the two stories following, connection and sharing are an intrinsic part of the mix.

Mother-daughter "girls night out"

The idea behind the "mother-daughter girl's night out" was for it to be a regular time for our kids to get together, while we (the moms) could also check in with each other. We would see each other briefly at school before that—drop-offs, and pick-ups, but never with enough time to really compare notes on what was going on at school, with our kids developmentally and socially. So these dinners provided a regular opportunity to connect, in a relaxed setting.

We chose to have them at affordable restaurants. We acknowledged that even if we rotated homes, it might just be too much to make a big dinner and clean up afterwards. We also wanted our daughters to see this as a special night for them. The girls got their own table, which made them feel very grown up, while giving them an opportunity to behave well in public. They were pleased to be "on their own," but usually, by the end of the meal, they pushed into our table, with all of us talking and laughing.

—Lisa Ross

Meditation groups: Leslie and three other women meet each Wednesday morning before work to participate in a group meditation, rotating among one another's homes. Individually, none had sufficient motivation to meditate alone; doing so in tandem has helped keep their commitment to the practice. They begin by checking in with one another to briefly discuss the issues on their minds. A seated meditation follows, usually from thirty to forty minutes, focusing on the breath. Sometimes Leslie asks a question of herself and finds that it is answered during the meditation. In the company of others, these women are able to find more focus for their practice.

Another meditation group meets at Shana's home once a month. They begin with a simple Japanese-style tea, then pull an "angel card" to give them a focus upon which to meditate (the angel cards contain a single word, such as *responsibility, adventure, acceptance,* etc.). After meditating for twenty to thirty minutes, there is a discussion to share some of the issues and awareness that surfaced during the meditation.

Walking and talking: On walks with friends, conversation flows and much terrain can be covered. Everyone wants more exercise, and meeting regularly with a friend to walk and talk is one of the best ways to keep one's own body as well as the friendship active. The benefits of walking are legion: increasing energy, clearing the mind, calming the spirit, and feeding the senses with the sights, sounds, and scents of the outdoors.

Marian and Teri have been walking together in the wee hours of the morning for more than seven years. Living just a few homes apart in a quiet neighborhood, they leave their homes at 6:00 a.m.—or earlier—seven days a week, dark or light, rain (even snow!) or shine. Mostly, their walks include talking; when silence falls, it's a companionable one. At the time of our interview, Marian's four children ranged in age from three to twelve; Teri's two sons were seven and nine. I can't help but feel awed by their commitment to this early morning ritual—I live in the same neighborhood and I have trouble enough prying myself out of bed at 6:00 a.m. just to go down to the kitchen, particularly on cold, dark winter mornings!

If I don't have friends, then I don't have nothing.
—Billie Holiday

When one of them is away or on vacation, Marian misses this walking-and-talking ritual. She finds it centers her and helps her pull her thoughts together before the madness of the day begins. If something is on her mind, this is her time to vent.

Cultural or intellectual pursuits: If your busy life leaves you feeling that your intellect could use some polishing, what better way to do so than with like-minded friends? Find a cozy yet accommodating public space or rotate among homes to meet and chat in a foreign language, discuss local or national issues, or explore the arts together. Jan gets together with six other women in her neighborhood one Sunday evening each month to discuss controversial issues. The women, who all live within walking distance from one another, call their group "the provocatives," and feel that, though they are mostly on the same page politically, the issues they discuss encourage dialog. The woman hosting that month's meeting chooses the topic, which can emerge from a chapter of a book, or a magazine or newspaper article with a controversial point of view. Occasionally, instead of meeting at a home, the women see an edgy play or museum exhibit together, then discuss it afterwards.

Knitting groups: Knitting groups are the contemporary answer to quilting circles. Not that the latter have gone away; far from it—the quilting circle has enjoyed quite a revival in the last twenty-five years. For women who wish to convene around the time-honored activity of socializing while working with one's hands, knitting groups offer a flexible, moveable option. Like quilting circles, knitting groups have long been around, but after September 11, 2001, they proliferated in unexpected numbers and attracted to their fold not only baby boomers but a generation of younger women. In fact, the Craft Yarn Council of America estimates that knitters under the age of thirty-five have increased by 50 percent since 1998. No longer the domain of grandmas-to-be knitting booties in a quiet corner, contemporary knitting groups create a form of community whose appeal is decidedly modern.

A modern network of knitters, congregating in all corners of New York City and Boston, has the gritty moniker of "Stitch 'n' Bitch" (there is also a knitter's guide with the same name—and attitude). Members are invited to convene in cafés or even bars to help one another work on projects while chatting, eating, and drinking. There are those who call knitting "the new yoga," referring to its meditative or centering effects. Most knitting groups gather for relaxation and camaraderie, but some convene for charitable purposes, creating blankets, robes, pillows, slippers, and other useful items for hospital patients and nursing homes.

Karen describes her neighborhood knitting and sewing group as "just coming together in an impromptu way after a few of us were lamenting that we start needlework projects—knitting, quilting, sewing, embroidery—but never seem to have a chance to finish them. One woman took the initiative to suggest that we meet every month or so at her house." This group, with four regulars and two more women who have been invited, range in age from about thirty to forty. "We talk about our projects and about the materials we prefer to work with," says Karen. Most have several projects going at once—a fantastic multicolored sweater, a baby blanket (hand sewn), a fancy scarf made from ribbon, a pair of socks, a fanciful quilt intended as a wedding present, a baby hat. After comparing notes on projects, the group segues into more personal realms: "We discuss pets, kids, the yard, the house, and work; and since the group is hosted by a British woman, we drink tea and eat scones." Karen always has a myriad of responsibilities to juggle, and finds that the knitting group is a perfect way to unwind, summing its appeal up simply: "I anticipate lots of fun when we meet."

Knitting groups are great for on-the-go women, combining moveable creativity with connection. To find one near you, your local yarn shop is a good bet; some libraries organize them, and the internet lists regional resources.

Friendship reunions: Friends that live a fair but not terribly long distance from one another can arrange a yearly reunion in an equidistant hotel. Abby and her dearest college friends, Elisa and Laura, live within two hours of one another, but their lives don't easily intersect. After graduation, they talked on the phone frequently, but as the years passed and their paths diverged, they kept in touch less and less. To keep their friendship intact, they decided to meet around midsummer every year for a weekend, either at a hotel or spa in a location centrally located to all of them. On a recent reunion, they all stayed in Abby's home for the first time, and she enjoyed being a tourist in her own town in the company of her good friends.

An old friend helps reflect our true selves back to us, those carefree girls we were once upon a time. See if you can organize a ritual for reuniting with old friends, even if for one day a year; it almost goes without saying that it will do you a world of good.

Clothing swap: Gathering a group of friends to participate in a clothing swap is a fabulous way to cure fashion ruts, clear out your closet, and enjoy a friendship ritual that's practical as well as fun. While trying on a friend's size 8 pants that no longer fit her, you also stand to gain some sisterly advice on what colors and styles look great on you (or not so great, as the case may be). The ideal time to organize a clothing swap is right around the time of the semiannual clothing switch in your closet—usually occurring in late spring and/or early fall. It's an ideal incentive to weed out the wardrobe and make room in the closet. To enhance the ritual, a potluck lunch or dinner preceding the swap can be a great ice breaker. Otherwise, it can be accompanied by an afternoon coffee or tea.

A successful swap works best if at least six women of fairly similar size participate. Though there is a certain intimacy to an exchange of clothing, participants can be encouraged to bring friends, to inject new energy and unfamiliar clothing. A good way to start the proceedings is

to have everyone sort through the clothing together, and group them by like items—pants can be draped over a certain couch, sweaters arranged on an open patch of clean carpet, and so on. This helps get everyone in the mood and start thinking about pieces they'd like to try on. Much of the fun is trying on styles or outfits that you've admired on others but feared were not really "you," and being open to comments and suggestions by other participants.

Some clothing swap groups put (reasonable) price tags on the clothing, and participants actually buy the clothing they want (bargaining is allowed!). The proceeds are then pooled and the money donated to a charity agreed upon in advance. Clothing swap fund-raisers often favor charities that benefit women, such as a shelter. The proceeds, as well as any unbought clothing, can be donated in tandem.

Most clothing swappers come away from an evening of camaraderie with at least a couple of new outfits and the good feeling of having passed along clothing to be enjoyed by another.

Biannual clothing swap

We're a group of six old friends living in a small college town. We started out as a mom's group when our kids were babies and toddlers, and now, between us, we have thirteen teenagers, eight of whom are girls. Two of us are divorced and one remarried, so it's impossible to get all the families together—too complicated, and too many people!

Twice a year, usually April and October, the six of us get together for a clothing swap and most of our daughters love to participate. Wanda, who has a great rec room in her basement, is gracious enough to host the event each time. We start out by having a dessert buffet; everyone brings a dessert or fruit salad to share and Wanda sets out a pot of coffee and provides the dishes and cups.

We set up the women's clothing on one side of the room, and the girls' clothing on the other. We have a blast trying on each other's clothing, and the girls just love it—you know how teenage girls are with clothing. If they know they're going to come away with some free outfits, you don't have to ask them twice to come along. Any unclaimed clothes get donated to the local Junior League for their hospital thrift shop. This is a great event that helps us stay connected as a group. And it's amazing how one person's fashion mistake can be just right for a friend!

—Beverly Jamelin

Sensible Executive

Earth Mother

Simple ideas for standing dates with friends

Girlfriend adventures: Gather a group of friends and meet once a month to enjoy the outdoors together. Take a long hike, or go biking or kayaking. Pack a picnic and savor your time together, as well as the peace of being out in the natural world.

Monthly museum visits: How often do you take advantage of museums within a one-hour radius of where you live? Hmmm, I thought so. Designate one afternoon a month to meet with friends at various museums (art, science, historical) in your area. Bring your kids once in a while, or make a museum outing a kid-friendly ritual to begin with. Treat yourselves to coffee or tea in the museum's café to discuss what you've seen.

Grow a garden group: Garden lovers can plan monthly visits to gardens of all kinds, whether a formal garden, arboretum, or botanical garden. In cooler months, visit greenhouses and great garden shops. Those with a passion for plants can glean ideas for their own gardens, or simply enjoy this as an occasion to absorb beauty.

Film friends: Once a month, gather your girlfriends to see an independent or foreign film, and allow time afterwards for a discussion. Or for something a little less highbrow, get together for a "chick flick" night in one of your homes, for a movie that male partners wouldn't be caught dead watching.

Volunteering in tandem: Like meditating, volunteering in our communities is something many of us feel we should do, but never seem to find time for. Volunteering on a regular basis with a friend or a group of friends creates a ritual around this activity, and you may find more incentive in doing good together (see one such story on page 42).

Writing in cafés: In her classic *Writing Down the Bones,* Natalie Goldberg often mentions meeting friends in cafés to write together over coffee or lunch. Aspiring writers can meet in a café once a week or twice a month and write together, either as a way to get some work done, fueled by group energy, to share and critique, or both.

Shared creative time: Many women wish they had more time for creative pursuits. Designate a regular ritual for creativity with your friends. Take a local trip with your group to photograph, sketch, or watercolor; seek out short workshops to attend together; sit in a cozy living room and work on fiber arts (see Knitting groups, page 116).

Structure a ritual around physical activity: Perhaps there is so much resistance around the concept of exercise because it's often such a lonely business. Creating a ritual around physical activity makes it less daunting and helps everyone stay on task. Regular walks with friends (see Walking and talking, page 114) is perhaps one of the simplest ways to connect and move your body at the same time. Or consider ice-skating, swimming, taking a dance class, or attending a yoga or Pilates class with a friend or two, then going out for a healthy meal afterwards.

Resources

Girlfriend Gatherings: Creative Ways to Stay Connected by Janet Holm McHenry (Harvest House Publishers, 2001) is a simple little book filled with ways to foster and maintain "girlfriend" connections between old and new friends, neighbors, former roommates, and classmates.

The Red Hat Society: Fun and Friendship After 50 by Sue Ellen Cooper (Warner Books, 2004) is by a woman who was inspired to host social gatherings for over-50 women, who she felt could be sometimes invisible in our culture. The idea is to gather and do fun things, preferably dressed flamboyantly for these occasions. After all, this trend was inspired by the poem, "when I am an old woman I shall wear purple/with a red hat that doesn't suit me. . . ."

Join (or start) a women's book group

My friend Jan participated in one of the first book groups I had ever heard about, long before it became trendy. Was I envious! Would that we lived in the same state, I too would have loved to be a book group pioneer. From the start, Jan's group had a focus, choosing to read women authors only, and used the books' themes as launching points for examining personal issues. Women's spirituality and controversial subjects were favorites, as those inspired the most provocative discussions. Though the group disbanded after eight solid years, the core members enjoy continued friendships and a twice-a-year dinner reunion.

These days, I know as many women as not who belong to a book group. While book groups can be most rewarding for anyone, male or female, single or part of a family, for those of us who are busy with kids, it is a perfect little escape. The combination of intellectual stimulation and regular get-togethers with like-minded friends is unbeatable. Book groups can motivate you to do quality reading at times when doing so seems most challenging. These convivial meetings of the mind offer not only food for thought, but opportunities for connection and friendship.

So often, after turning the last page of a wonderful book, I longed to extend the experience with a spirited discussion. With no success locating a suitable existing group, I finally bit the bullet and formed one of my own (somewhat reluctantly, as by nature I'm not an organizer), designating a meeting just once every six weeks to accommodate busy schedules and slower readers. It's not hard to start a book group, once you make up your mind to do so.

Begin by finding three or four book lovers, and ask each to bring one like-minded friend. Eight or ten is a good number. At any given meeting there may be those who can't attend, but a group of at least five or six can make for a good discussion. While many groups like to keep their selections eclectic, others like to maintain a focus or play with various themes or formats. Many book groups stay with a tightly focused theme at least for some time, if not its duration.

World affairs, science fiction and fantasy, children's literature, foreign language books, and food and travel are just a few areas on which reading groups concentrate. Having a focus helps when a group is just getting started. Following are a few ideas to get you started. Chances are, if you and your group put your minds together, you'll come up with others.

Nonfiction themes: When my book group was just starting to gel, some of our fiction selections fell short of expectations. We switched to discussing themes rather than books until we got to know one another better. Everyone got to read a book of their own choosing on the selected theme; afterwards, we would swap books. Our discussions on the subjects of Feng Shui, travel memoirs, and the simplicity movement were fun as well as enlightening.

Some say life's the thing,
but me, I prefer to read.

—Logan Pearsall Smith

Focus on females: If you had your fill of male authors in school, you may want to consider a focus on classic women writers, as Rebecca's book group does. They've read books by Willa Cather, Gertrude Stein, Virginia Woolf, Zora Neal Thurston, Vita Sackville-West, and others. Rebecca and her friends consider their literary experience greatly enhanced by female voices. Jan's group, mentioned earlier, also stayed exclusively with female authors, fiction and nonfiction.

Reading and eating: This duo of passions can become one delicious ritual, combining your discussions with a potluck dinner, brunch, or dessert buffet. An increasing number of book groups are doing so. Take these pleasures to new heights by choosing books with a culinary theme, and pairing them with your food selections—earthy Mexican food and *Like Water for Chocolate;* homemade chocolate treats with *Chocolat;* rustic French fare with *A Year in Provence.* The possibilities are endless—and highly appetizing.

Lunch hour book group: Those with truly crowded schedules might want to take a page from a professional women's book group in Washington, D.C. They convene once a month in a museum café, taking a slightly longer-than-usual lunch break to discuss the Pulitzer Prize winning books that are the focus of their selections.

Book group field trips: Enrich your reading group experience by taking field trips or occasional "pilgrimages." Plan a literary adventure for your group as an exciting, once-a-year event. Is there a well-known author's or historic figure's home within driving range? Within a three-hour radius of my group's home base, for instance, are the dwellings of the Roosevelts, Mark Twain, Edith Wharton, Washington Irving, and Emily Dickinson. All are open to the public. Do some research to discover which authors once lived in your region. Read their writings and/or a biography, then voyage en masse to pay homage to your local luminaries.

Women's biographies: Sarah's group shares a love for biographies of accomplished or daring women. This past year their selections have included Georgia O'Keefe, Amelia Earhart, Mae West, Billie Holiday, and collected biographies of "women of the wild west." On their agenda are Cleopatra, Martha Graham, Edna St. Vincent Millay, and Colette. "Their lives were never tidy and not always happy, but they always followed their unique paths, even if it meant breaking the rules," Sarah explains. "We gain tremendous insights from their courage, especially when we're feeling wimpy."

*No sooner did I realize I
was likely to grow up to be
a woman than I wanted to
know what the possibilities
were for women's lives. . . .
I wanted wild women,
women who broke loose,
women who lived life to the
full.*

—Phyllis Rose,
*The Norton Book of
Women's Lives*

Mother's play group/book club

When my children were young, I was involved in a combination play group and book club. While the moms discussed our books, the kids played together. I found this a wonderful antidote to "cotton brain" syndrome. Not that there weren't interruptions—one kid would need a diaper change, another would cry when it got too hard to share toys. We made sure to choose books that were fairly short and didn't require huge amounts of concentration, so we managed to read one good book a month, a great accomplishment for women with one or two small children.

We got together every two weeks, and during the "in between" week when we didn't actually discuss the book, we at least had a progress report to make sure everyone was into the book. If everyone hated it, we'd change rather than stay committed to a book that we were just slogging through. Our reading time was just too precious for that.

We rotated among our homes, and everyone brought bagels and fruit and other goodies. I don't know what I would have done without the book group when my kids were toddlers. Possibly, I would have lost my mind.

—Nancy Gladstein

Resources

There are quite a number of good resources for aspiring book groups; they feature suggestions for good reading group books, discussion techniques, logistical matters, and more. Look for book group guides on individual publisher's web sites. Here is a selected list of books on the subject:

Good Books Lately: The One-Stop Resource for Book Groups and Other Greedy Readers by Ellen Moore and Kira Stevens (St. Martin's Griffin, 2004) not only lists good book group selections, but has lots of tips on starting and maintaining groups. A unique feature is that this book addresses the issue of how to inject new energy into book group discussions that have become dull.

The Book Club Cookbook: Recipes and Food for Thought from Your Book Club's Favorite Books and Authors by Judy Gelmand and Vicki Levy Krupp (Jeremy P. Tarcher, 2004). This clever book group cookbook gleans food-related passages from a wide selection of books and pairs them with recipes.

The Book Group Book: A Thoughtful Guide to Forming and Enjoying a Stimulating Book Discussion Group by Ellen Slezak (Chicago Review Press, 2000) is a practical guide that is revised and updated every few years.

The lost art of letter writing

You've got mail—e-mail, that is. Aren't you excited? Of course you're not. These days, receiving and answering e-mail is about as exciting as brushing your teeth—just a mundane daily task. Now, if you had gotten real mail, an honest to goodness handwritten letter on lovely stationary with an exotic stamp, I know you'd be excited. I would be, too—getting an actual letter from a real person is a very big deal, but rarely does one appear among the bills, credit card offers, coupons, and catalogs that clog my mailbox. Still, hope springs eternal, and I'm ever watchful for those elusive missives. I'd give anything for a letter addressed in loopy handwriting, with butterfly stamps—from a long lost friend, or anyone, really—living on some exotic island. After a particularly dry spell, I so missed getting personal letters that I simply set aside some time and sent out a round of actual, handwritten letters to friends and colleagues with whom I had not been in touch for some time.

A week or two went by, then—the results amazed me. A fellow author sent a signed copy of her most recent book. My college roommate wrote back with news of her adopted Chinese baby girl. A favorite high school buddy sent a postcard letting me know that he was going on a long journey to the Far East. Since he now had my address, more postcards followed from Nepal and Thailand ("The Land of Smiles"). I established a correspondence with an elderly former neighbor who sends gardening tips. Two writing colleagues chose to respond via e-mail. So did my best friend from elementary school. Not as much fun, but still, we reconnected.

I'll admit that my results were remarkably good. I can't guarantee the same for you, but why not give it a try? Writing a warm, personal letter to a friend is like sending a piece of your soul into the world. For the cost of a stamp, a portion of your personal energy takes a journey to a faraway place. Taking a few moments to write a letter is an exquisite way to spend quiet time alone; at the same time, it's an intimate way to share yourself with a kindred spirit.

A short, timely letter can enhance moments of your day: it can be a gem given or received. . . . The letter-writing ritual should be generously provided for. Sending a surprise letter to a friend is like sending your ship out to sail.

—Alexandra Stoddard
Living a Beautiful Life

Sending out letters in spurts is a nice way to receive letters back—in spurts. But if you'd like the lost art of letter writing to be a regular part of your life, you need to—you guessed it—establish some rituals around this gratifying activity.

Prepare your supplies: Establishing a letter-writing ritual is easier and more enjoyable if the supplies are right at hand. Prepare a small basket to keep in an accessible spot. Fill it with special writing pens, such as roller ball pens with smoothly flowing ink; blank cards or attractive note paper with matching envelopes; postcards; perhaps a handful of humorous cards; plus special-issue stamps for both first-class, postcard, and airmail rates. Whenever you travel or visit a museum, stock up on a few colorful postcards. A spiral address book adds the final flourish to your correspondence basket.

Correspond with an elderly friend: If there's little hope for corresponding with your too-busy, type-A friends, try establishing a regular correspondence with an elderly person. It's a small act of kindness that goes a long way. Those of the prewired generation can feel particularly left behind in this era of electronic communication. In turn, you're likely to receive handsomely scripted letters filled with genuine sentiment, family or neighborhood news, and old-fashioned wisdom.

Interfamily letters: Exchanging letters with those you live with is nearly as much fun (and sometimes more meaningful) than getting them in the mail. Love notes, lunch box notes, birthday letters (see page 53 for more on these), and other interfamily letter writing can be a wonderful way to enhance communication, and even resolve conflicts. Andrea and her longtime partner, Carl, both artists, create a postcard for one another each week. One side is a simple collage or drawing, and on the reverse, a short poem or message. This ritual is not only an exercise in creativity, but a reflection of the ups and downs of the couple's relationship. When it's going smoothly, the postcards are affirming and romantic. When the relationship hits a snag, the postcards can be cathartic and a stepping stone to dialog. The same can be done between parents and kids. Letters can be a thoughtful, non-threatening venue for exploring conflicts and expressing thoughts that can otherwise be awkward to convey verbally.

Pen-pals for kids: Children love to receive mail. Encourage them to find pen pals and establish a routine around the exchange of correspondence. Though numerous clubs are dedicated to pen pals, it may be best for children to correspond with someone you know personally. Cousins or other relatives in other parts of the country, friends and neighbors who have moved away, and distant grandparents are ideal correspondents. Help your child establish a letter-writing ritual with a letter-writing basket like yours. Let them select colorful stationery and postcards, as well as stickers and rubber stamps.

Letters as shared journals: If you've always wanted to keep a journal, but can't stay motivated, consider keeping a shared journal with a friend. It's an intimate form of shared correspondence. Jayne and Maxine, two old friends living on opposite coasts, did just that, using an interactive journal as an intimate form of letter writing. They literally sent a journal back and forth across the county for three years. In a series of lightweight notebooks that could be slipped into a 6-by-9-inch envelope, one woman would write her journal entry, her friend would first react to the entry, then write her own. This shared journal saw the friends through crises—a divorce, the death of a parent, the loss of a long-standing job—as well as joys, including the birth of a first grandchild and an exhilarating midlife romance. After the need for intense correspondence waned, the two women divided the notebooks between themselves as keepsakes.

Please give me some good advice in your next letter. I promise not to follow it.

—Edna St. Vincent Millay

Your pages: A rituals and traditions workbook

Hopefully, this book has given you much to ponder, many ideas, and inspiration for rituals and traditions that elevate ordinary living. Finally, though, what makes a ritual work is that you've made it your own. Not that it has to be completely unique or creative, but that it's just right for you and your family. Use these pages to record the rituals you already enjoy, think about ways to tweak your routines into rituals, and muse about rituals and traditions you'd like to establish. After each section there's also some room for notes and ideas to help you with planning. Use this space to jot down, for instance, names of people you'd like to take walks with (and maybe even their phone numbers and e-mails addresses), families you might contact to form a dinner club, places you'd like to visit regularly, or even books and web sites you read about in these pages that might inspire further ideas.

Personal rituals: What, when, and how often?

Your first step in recording and refining your rituals is to simply inventory them. Write your existing rituals as well as "almost-ritual" routines—make a simple "laundry list." This will give you a better idea of the things you do regularly. On the pages following each category, you can begin your wish list of rituals you'd like to establish, or at least try on for size.

As you think about the various kinds of rituals and traditions you and your family and friends already enjoy or want to try, remember that there are many things we do on a regular basis that feel more like routines, because we haven't given them much thought. Certain routines, like brushing your teeth or taking out the garbage, need to stay in the routine category. Others, though, can be elevated into ritual by giving them attention and some added flourish. What ordinary activities would you like to transform into rituals? Making and eating daily dinner, getting together with a particular group of friends, reading books, going for walks, or even going to sleep can be given just enough personal flair to become rituals.

Daily rituals: Include here rituals for mealtimes, hellos, goodbyes, good mornings, good nights, private time—anything you do on a daily basis. Don't worry if this one's a short list—no one can be expected to have lots of daily rituals.

Your daily rituals

Daily rituals wish list (with notes and resources) _____

Weekly rituals: Think about what you do to celebrate the end of a busy week or what you do for regular family fun. Do you have a family meeting, participate in regular volunteer activities, or shared physical activities? If you have special weekly meals, you can either record them here or in the section for food rituals on page 150.

Your weekly rituals _____

*Weekly rituals wish list (with notes and resources)*_____

Monthly rituals: Do you get together with your friends once a month for a specific purpose, like a book club or knitting group? Do you have a one-on-one evening out with one of your children? Does your family do a once-a-month outing to a nearby city, park, or museum?

Your monthly rituals _____

Monthly rituals wish list (with notes and resources) _____

Seasonal rituals: Are there particular activities your family enjoys or would enjoy doing each spring, summer, winter, and fall? Is there a vacation spot you return to each year, at a particular time of year? Are there nature activities you are drawn to doing each season? Do you acknowledge the winter or summer solstice?

Your spring rituals _____

_____

_____

_____

_____

_____

_____

_____

Spring rituals wish list _____

_____

_____

_____

_____

_____

_____

_____

_____

Your summer rituals

_____

_____

_____

_____

_____

_____

_____

_____

_____

_____

_____

Summer rituals wish list

_____

_____

_____

_____

_____

_____

_____

_____

_____

_____

Your fall rituals _____

_____

_____

_____

_____

_____

_____

_____

_____

_____

_____

Fall rituals wish list _____

_____

_____

_____

_____

_____

_____

_____

_____

_____

_____

Your winter rituals

Winter rituals wish list

Yearly rituals: Into this category fall birthdays, anniversaries and other celebrations, the big annual vacation, reunions, and such. You can also include offbeat things like celebrating Ground Hog Day, attending the county fair, or participating in an annual walkathon—anything that happens mainly once a year, but that has significance in your family's repertoire.

Your yearly rituals _____

Yearly rituals wish list (with notes and resources) _____

_____

_____

_____

_____

_____

_____

_____

_____

_____

_____

_____

_____

_____

_____

_____

_____

_____

_____

_____

_____

_____

_____

_____

_____

Holiday and special celebration rituals: We didn't spend a lot of time on traditional holiday rituals in this book. Still, since you're already thinking about your rituals, here's a handy place to record your favorite holiday traditions here. While doing so, you may even think of ways to make them better. Following these two pages is space for you to record the smaller celebrations and unique holidays you celebrate—or would like to celebrate—with your family and friends.

Your holiday traditions _____

_____

_____

_____

_____

_____

_____

_____

_____

_____

_____

_____

_____

_____

_____

_____

_____

Holiday traditions wish list (with notes and resources) _____

Smaller celebrations and unique celebrations

Small celebrations wish list _____

Food rituals and traditions: Many rituals, ordinary or celebratory, involve food. What food rituals are important to you? Are there particular seasonal foods you enjoy? Do you shop at an offbeat market each week? What are your family's favorite comfort foods? Do you have a "cooking together" ritual with family members or friends? Do you gather for regular meals with extended family, or participate in a dinner club?

Your food traditions _____

_____

_____

_____

_____

_____

_____

_____

_____

_____

_____

_____

_____

_____

_____

_____

_____

_____

Food traditions wish list _____

Rituals of remembrance: What rituals do you have in place that preserve your family's unique story? How do you celebrate milestones, rites of passage, "first and lasts" (such as the first day of a new grade, or the last day of soccer season) so that they will be remembered? Do you have a special way to record your children's growth and milestones, like a scrapbook, or a wall of photos that are taken in the same spot each year? Do you honor departed loved ones, or hold reunions to keep family stories alive?

Your rituals of remembrance _____

Rituals of remembrance wish list _____

_____

_____

_____

_____

_____

_____

_____

_____

_____

_____

_____

_____

_____

_____

_____

_____

_____

_____

_____

_____

_____

_____

Letting go of rituals: Sometimes, rituals reach their natural conclusion. A child no longer wants you to read to them at night (they'd rather lose themselves in chapter books); a combination Sunday brunch and family meeting dwindles with your teen's need to sleep late; your child no longer wants to bake with you on Saturday mornings, preferring instead to take karate or skateboard with friends. There's no set way to let go of rituals, except with grace, and with the acceptance that it's no longer a ritual once it feels more like an obligation. Sometimes, it helps to simply acknowledge that the ritual has reached its natural conclusion, and to put into words what was most enjoyable about it while it lasted. Here's a place for you to write about rituals past. Consider what they meant to you and/or your family, and how you felt when it was time to let them go.

Acknowledgments

This book was several years in the making. As this project draws to a close, I've begun to think of its creative process as akin to piecing together a patchwork quilt. I've gathered stories, ideas, quotations, my own experiences as a parent, and all sorts of bits and pieces from here and there. Many things were put in, taken out, and sometimes put in again. I've done numerous illustrations, torn some up, combined others, and rejected a few, only to find them useful at a later date. I've relied on many people in numerous ways, without whom this book would have been more like a monochromatic blanket than the colorfully stitched and richly varied quilt of words and images that it ultimately has become.

At the top of my list of acknowledgements is Lisa Ross, my agent. When we started working together, it was on a project that carried only the seed of this one. Lisa gently prodded me until I found a more coherent direction and a clearer voice. Ultimately, Lisa became the editor for this book, and I couldn't have asked for anyone who understands its essence more than she does. I also thank her for contributing a couple of her own favorite family ritual stories to these pages.

I am grateful to my husband, Harry Tabak, and my sons, Adam and Evan, for simply being the kind of people who appreciate the pleasures of home and who enjoy all the adventures we have, and have always had, as a family.

When I decided to try to design this book as well as write and illustrate it (something I had not done since before the era of computerized page layout), I did so with the support of the Visual Research Laboratory program at the State University of New York at New Paltz. I especially thank professors Ann Lovett and Clif Meador for their guidance as I bumbled through design issues like a rank beginner. I couldn't have gotten such a running start without Amy Papaellias, who tutored me in InDesign most patiently and contributed a family story to this book as well.

Many thanks to Gail Bradney for taking the all-important tasks of copy-editing and proof-reading and elevating them to an art form. And to Mary Neal Meador, thank you for seeing to it that my design blunders don't haunt me for the rest of my life.

Finally, I'd like to thank the many women who shared their stories of family rituals and traditions, in alphabetic order: Anne Atlas, Cynthia Aviles-Flores, Alicia Bayer (founder of the web site www. magical childhood.com), Marsha Berkower, Terry Morales Betts, Jennifer Bonnar, Leslie Cerier, Becky Calfin Chen, Janet Crawshaw (Co-founder, *The Valley Table* magazine), Carolyn Davis and her daughter, Chelsea Bleckwehl, Sylvia Diaz, Beth Ehrenberg, Stacie Flint, Jenny Friedman, Maya Talisman Frost, Jayne Galiano, Ellen Galinsky (president of Families and Work Institute), Nancy Gladstein, Jan Goldstein, Carlie Graves, Alison Greenberg, Gayil Greene, Katherine, Annie, and Peggy Happel, Olive Harris, Geetha Murthy Holdsworth, Deb Horowitz, Lee Iden, Amanda Jackson, Beverly Jamilan, Shana Klimpel, Deborah Kneff, Marian Liggera, Wendy Lipstein, Barbara McPhail, Reed Mangels, Sarah Margolin, Gina Luna Maserjian, Andrea Miller, Leah and Robin Moskowitz, Lisa Newman, Karen Nichols, Maggie Panzera, Kate Reese, Karen Robillard, Martina Rodriguez-Ward, Mary Rogers, Abby Saxon, Maxine Ann Sharma, Susan Shaughnessy, Christine Whittager Sofge, Iza Trapani (author of *The Itsy-Bitsy Spider, I'm a Little Teapot,* and many other delightful books for young children), Melanie Wilson (editor, *vegetarianbaby.com* and *vegetarianteen.com*), Barbara Zimmerman-Klein, and Susan Zucker. Special thanks to HarperCollins Publishers for permission to reprint the story of celebrating Mozart's birthday from *Shelter for the Spirit: Create Your Own Haven in a Hectic World* (1998) by Victoria Moran.

Bibliography

Many books and web sites for exploring varioius topics further are listed under the Resources sections throughtout the book. Here is a selection of books for more general reading relating to the topics of family ritual, tradition, and home life.

Biziou, Barbara. *The Joys of Everyday Ritual: Spiritual Recipes to Celebrate Milestones, Ease Transitions, and Make Every Day Sacred.* NY: St. Martin's Griffin, 1999

Biziou, Barbara. *The Joy of Family Ritual: Recipes for Everyday Living.* NY: St. Martin's Press, 2000

Cox, Meg. *The Heart of a Family: Searching America for New Traditions That Fulfill Us.* NY: Random House, 1998

Cox, Meg. *The Book of New Family Traditions: How to Create Great Rituals for Holidays and Everydays.* Philadelphia: Running Press, 2003

Doe, Mimi. *Busy but Balanced: Practical and Inspirational Ways to Create a Calmer, Closer Family.* NY: St. Martin's Press, 2001

Davis, Rondi Hillstrom and Oakes, Janell Sewall. *Together: Creating Family Traditions.* Dallas, TX: Nine Twenty Press, 2002

Doherty, William J., Ph.D. *The Intentional Family: Simple Rituals to Strengthen Family Ties.* NY: Quill/HarperCollins, 1997

Imber-Black, Evan, and Roberts, Janine. *Rituals for Our Times: Celebrating, Healing, and Changing Our Lives and Our Relationships.* Lanham, MD: Rowman & Littlefield Publishing Group, 1998

Johnson, Cait. *Witch in the Kitchen: Magical Cooking for All Seasons.* Rochester, VT: Destiny Books, 2001

Johnson, Cait, and Shaw, Maura D. *Celebrating the Great Mother: A Handbook of Earth-Honoring Activities for Parents and Children.* Rochester, VT: Destinty Books, 1995

Lieberman, Susan Abel. *New Traditions: Redefining Celebrations for Today's Family*. NY: Noonday Press/ Farrar Straus Giroux, 1991

Luhrs, Janet. *The Simple Living Guide: A Sourcebook for Less Stressful, More Joyful Living*. NY: Broadway Books, 1997

Moran, Victoria. *Shelter For the Sprit: Create Your Own Haven in a Hectic World*. NY: Perennial Books, 1998

Nelson, Gertrud Mueller. *To Dance With God: Family Ritual and Community Celebration*. Mahwah, NJ: Paulist Press, 1986

Robertson, Robin, and Robertson, Jon. *The Sacred Kitchen: Higher-Consciousness Cooking for Health and Wholeness*. Novato, CA: New World Library, 1999

Scott, Anne. *Serving Fire: Food for Thought, Body, and Soul.*Berkeley, CA: Celestial Arts, 1994

Stoddard, Alexandra. *Living a Beautiful Life: 500 Ways to Add Elegance, Order, Beauty, and Joy to Every Day of Your Life*. NY: Avon Books, 1986

Share your rituals!

For the *Everyday Traditions* website, I invite readers to share their favorite ritual stories with me and other readers. How did the rituals and traditions you most enjoy with your family and friends start; how have they evolved? Be as detailed as you'd like, since your stories can help not only continue the thoughts and ideas started in these pages, but will surely inspire others to create their own rituals and traditions. Send your stories and anecdotes to me at nava@everydaytraditions.com.